S. HRG. 115–210

MAKING INDIAN COUNTRY COUNT: NATIVE AMERICANS AND THE 2020 CENSUS

HEARING

BEFORE THE

COMMITTEE ON INDIAN AFFAIRS
UNITED STATES SENATE

ONE HUNDRED FIFTEENTH CONGRESS

SECOND SESSION

FEBRUARY 14, 2018

Printed for the use of the Committee on Indian Affairs

U.S. GOVERNMENT PUBLISHING OFFICE

29–840 PDF   WASHINGTON : 2018

For sale by the Superintendent of Documents, U.S. Government Publishing Office
Internet: bookstore.gpo.gov Phone: toll free (866) 512–1800; DC area (202) 512–1800
Fax: (202) 512–2104 Mail: Stop IDCC, Washington, DC 20402–0001

CONTENTS

MAKING INDIAN COUNTRY COUNT: NATIVE AMERICANS AND THE 2020 CENSUS

WEDNESDAY, FEBRUARY 14, 2018

U.S. SENATE,
COMMITTEE ON INDIAN AFFAIRS,
Washington, DC.

The Committee met, pursuant to notice, at 2:59 p.m. in room 628, Dirksen Senate Office Building, Hon. John Hoeven, Chairman of the Committee, presiding.

OPENING STATEMENT OF HON. JOHN HOEVEN, U.S. SENATOR FROM NORTH DAKOTA

The CHAIRMAN. I also have to say, in regard to the business meeting, that I ask unanimous consent that staff be allowed to make technical and conforming changes, which we can do as long as the Vice Chairman agrees that we allow them to do it.

Senator UDALL. No objection.

The CHAIRMAN. All right. Thank you, Vice Chairman Udall.

We will proceed now with our hearing, and I want to thank all of the witnesses for being with us today.

Good afternoon. I call this oversight hearing to order. Today the Committee will hold an oversight hearing on the upcoming 2020 Census.

Our Constitution requires that our Nation's population be accurately counted every 10 years. However, in Indian Country, getting an accurate population count can be a difficult task. Many tribal communities are located in geographically isolated areas. Among other challenges, simply accessing these communities can inhibit an accurate census count.

Although it may be difficult to collect census data, it is critical for our Nation. Census results are used to draw district lines for the U.S. House of Representatives, State legislatures, and local governments. They determine the distribution of $600 billion in annual Federal assistance to States, localities, and to Tribes. They also direct community decisions affecting schools, housing, transportation, and healthcare services. All of these functions are dependent on an accurate census.

To ensure an accurate count in Indian Country, the Census Bureau must continue to engage in meaningful outreach with tribal communities to find innovative solutions. In 2015 and 2016, the Census Bureau held a series of consultation sessions with tribal communities. The Bureau issued a final report on these consulta-

(1)

tion sessions, which includes recommendations on how to accurately count American Indians and Alaska Natives.

In my home State of North Dakota, there are roughly 32,000 Native Americans and, because of the strong presence of Native Americans in my State, one of the Bureau's consultation sessions was conducted in Fort Yates, North Dakota. I look forward to hearing about the Bureau's progress in addressing recommendations from Tribes in North Dakota and across the Country, as well as how the Administration, Tribes, and other stakeholders can work together to conduct an accurate count of the Native American community in the upcoming 2020 Census.

With that, I want to welcome our witnesses. Thank you for being here, and I look forward to your testimony.

Before we hear from the witnesses, I want to turn to Vice Chairman Udall for his opening statement.

STATEMENT OF HON. TOM UDALL, U.S. SENATOR FROM NEW MEXICO

Senator UDALL. Thank you, Chairman Hoeven, for holding this important oversight hearing on the census. With 2020 around the corner and preparations already underway, it is very timely to be doing so.

And thank you to the witnesses today for coming out to shed light on a topic that will impact Indian Country for years to come.

Administering the census is a task so fundamental to how our government operates that our Nation's founders included it in the Constitution. With far-reaching consequences, our founders' decision was for a good reason. Valid and accurate census data is the bedrock of fair, proportionate representation in our democracy. The census's detailed demographic data is used to implement the Voting Rights Act. An inaccurate census risks underrepresentation for tribal communities, and an undercount can lead to skewed State, local, and Federal voting districts that diminish the voices of those communities.

The census has a big impact on Indian Country when it comes to voting, one or our most essential civil rights. Basic obligations like language assistance at the polls and voter registration in tribal communities' own language can be influenced by an undercount, and Federal agencies rely on the census and American community survey data when enforcing civil rights laws.

The results of the census have a ripple effect beyond just the government. Businesses look at these population estimates when looking to expand, and they influence how communities, including Tribes, plan for schools and hospitals. That makes it all the more important that we get the census right. Unfortunately, the Bureau certainly hasn't in the past. In 1990, the census undercounted the American Indian population on reservations by 12 percent; then undercounted that population again in 2010 by 5 percent.

I am concerned that funding shortfalls leading to the cancellation of important field tests are only further straining the Bureau's ability to carry out this constitutionally-mandated duty. This has very real consequences for Indian Country; census data determines how the government will distribute more than $600 billion this year, and more than \$6 trillion over the next 10 years, by some estimates.

Putting those numbers in context, in New Mexico, the Federal Government spends about \$3,000 per person on everything from how the government distributes Medicaid dollars and SNAP funds to tribal transportation and housing. That means for every person the census misses, thousands of dollars are lost. In a budget environment where Indian Country is already underfunded, we can't afford to let these dollars leave Indian Country.

I am glad, Mr. Chairman, that we are holding this hearing to make sure the Bureau gets the census right this time around.

With that, I look forward to hearing from our witnesses about the outlook for this year, with the eye towards 2020. Thank you.

The CHAIRMAN. Thank you, Vice Chairman Udall.

Now we will hear from our witnesses. They are Mr. Ron S. Jarmin, Associate Director for Economic Programs, and Performing the Non-Exclusive Functions and Duties of the Director of the U.S. Census Bureau here in Washington, D.C.; Ms. Carol Gore, President and Chief Executive Officer, Cook Inlet Housing, Anchorage, Alaska; the Honorable Jefferson Keel, President, National Congress of American Indians; Mr. James T. Tucker, Pro Bono Voting Rights Counsel, Native American Rights Fund, Las Vegas, Nevada.

Also, before we proceed with the witnesses, I understand, Senator Heitkamp, you would like to make some opening remarks?

STATEMENT OF HON. HEIDI HEITKAMP,
U.S. SENATOR FROM NORTH DAKOTA

Senator HEITKAMP. Thank you, Mr. Chairman. I want to mention the work that is being done in our other committee, Homeland Security and Government Affairs.

So, Mr. Jarmin, it is good to see you. This is an issue that is near and dear to my heart because it is so critically important that we get these counts right. And as I told Secretary Ross in October that there should be a series of hearings concerning the Census Bureau and the plan for the 2020, not just on this unique population.

Also, HSGAC is waiting to hear back from the secretary regarding his response to the Committee's questions for the record from our October hearing. October was a long time ago, I might remind you. If you could pass that along, it would be greatly appreciated.

Simply put, the 2020 Census I think, quite frankly, never mind this issue, is in trouble. Cancelled tests, increasing costs projections, and no Senate-confirmed director are all signs that the operation is teetering. We can get this back on track, but we are running out of time, so there is some urgency that I feel about this issue. So I am pleased and grateful that the Chairman and the Vice Chairman are taking a closer look at the challenges of enumerating folks in Indian Country.

Indian Reservations provide a unique challenge for the Census Bureau, such as historic distrust of the Federal Government, so when you knock on the door, they don't always answer and they don't always tell you who is there; a lower likelihood of deliverable mail, another issue that we are trying to solve; and sparse population centers. For too long we have given Indian Country the leftovers. Members of these communities, our first Americans, deserve to be counted as Americans.

So I want answers to the questions about the status of the entire census and where we are and how we are going to get there. But this is an issue that we have the ability to do some tests. Standing Rock Sioux Nation was one of those test areas. That didn't happen because of budget cuts. So, it is critically important in our oversight role on this Committee and also on Homeland Security and Government Affairs that we get answers today, because the longer this goes, the deeper the well will be that we will have to climb out of, and the less likely we will be able to take corrections.

So thank you, Mr. Jarmin, for coming, and thanks to all the witnesses.

And, again, my great appreciation for this opportunity to speak, but also, Mr. Chairman, for your attention to this very, very important issue.

The CHAIRMAN. Thank you, Senator Heitkamp.

STATEMENT OF HON. LISA MURKOWSKI, U.S. SENATOR FROM ALASKA

Senator MURKOWSKI. Very briefly, Mr. Chairman. I want to thank you for this very important hearing. I think we all recognize that getting a complete census and accurate count is truly important. We recognize that this is an economic tool, and, when you undercount, then there are consequences that kind of ripple throughout, so making sure that we get it right and get it right the first time is important. As Senator Heitkamp has noted, there are challenges as we try to get an accurate count within Indian Country.

We have geography challenges in Alaska; access is tough, and making sure that we are not able only to gain physical access but, again, the mail service that Senator Heitkamp has mentioned, we have complex organizational and government structure with the Tribes, the tribal organizations, regional corporations, the village corporations, the bureaus and cities, it makes it perhaps even more complicated. But we have some good folks working together. We have Foraker Group, who has been working with us to get a good count. We have the Alaska Census Working Group, consisting of a lot of good strong leaders that are helping us particularly in our very, very rural areas.

But I want to welcome and thank the Committee for inviting Carol Gore, who has worked very, very hard on this issue. I have known her for a long time. As you mentioned, she is President of Cook Inlet Housing. She also serves as the Vice Chair of the Census Bureau's National Advisory Committee. We have worked with her on a number of issues. She is no stranger to the Committee, but I really appreciate her perspective and the value that she brings to the Committee, and I welcome her back to Washington.

Thank you, Mr. Chairman.

The CHAIRMAN. Mr. Jarmin.

STATEMENT OF RON S. JARMIN, ASSOCIATE DIRECTOR FOR ECONOMIC PROGRAMS, PERFORMING THE NON–EXCLUSIVE FUNCTIONS AND DUTIES OF THE DIRECTOR, U.S. CENSUS BUREAU

Mr. JARMIN. Good afternoon, Chairman Hoeven, Vice Chairman Udall, and members of the Committee. I welcome the opportunity to speak with you today about the Census Bureau's work to ensure a high-quality enumeration of American Indian and Alaska Native communities in the upcoming 2020 Census. I am excited to discuss our ongoing government-to-government relationships with our tribal partners and our collaborative efforts to plan a census that will count everyone, both on and off tribal lands, once, only once, and in the right place.

To help us prepare for the census, we have received vital insights and advice from the American Indian and Alaska Native community. We held a series of invaluable consultations with tribal leaders across the Nation; we meet monthly with tribal representatives; and we have continued our ongoing engagements with the Census Bureau's National Advisory Committee on racial, ethnic, and other populations.

The Advisory Committee has included several distinguished representatives of the Nation's American Indian and Alaska Native communities, including my fellow witnesses and trusted Census Bureau partners. We continue to implement and expand these critical partnerships.

Since 2015, we have traveled throughout the Country to meet with delegates representing over 250 Tribes and tribal corporations and organizations. I want to recognize a couple of the folks that have been key to that. I have Dee Alexander and Jamie Christy behind me, who, along with dozens of other staff from our headquarters and field organizations, have been tireless in their efforts to improve the count on Indian land.

In these consultations, we have heard a common concern that the Internet response is not a viable option in remote areas. To address this issue, we have used information from the American Community Survey and from the Federal Communications Commission to identify areas with low connectivity. We plan to mail or hand-deliver questionnaires to households in these areas, as well as provide the opportunity to respond via the telephone.

Tribal representatives have also expressed a strong interest in effective communications with Census Bureau field staff. We are committed to ensuring that the Census Bureau provides clear guidance and training, recognizing the unique preferences and challenges amongst these diverse tribal communities. Importantly, we will work together to recruit and hire members of American Indian and Alaska Native communities to manage and conduct field operations to encourage response.

The National Congress of American Indians voiced serious concerns regarding a proposal to include a tribal enrollment question on the 2020 Census due to concerns about privacy and tribal sovereignty. With their feedback, the Census Bureau has decided not to proceed with the tribal enrollment question. To date, more than 50 Tribes and related associations have already appointed a 2020 Census tribal liaison to work with our regional partnership staff, and we look forward to working with them to develop effective census promotional and outreach materials.

The Census Bureau is planning a robust, integrated partnership in communications campaign. An important component of this will be customized marketing and communications strategies and materials for use by our tribal partners. Assisting us in this task will be G&G Advertising, a nationally recognized leader in tailored outreach to American Indian and Alaska Native audiences, and a veteran of two previous decennial census advertising campaigns.

We continue to work with tribal governments to confirm and update legal geographic boundaries and address lists, and we receive updated information from them every year as part of the Boundary and Annexation Survey. While nearly half of tribal governments participated in 2017, we hope to improve participation in 2018 by increasing our follow-up with those who haven't yet responded.

So far, more than 130 tribal governments have registered to review and update the Census Bureau's address lists and maps as part of the Local Update of Census Addresses Program, or LUCA, and we are on track to kick off the enumeration in Alaska on January 20th of 2020. We begin enumeration earlier in these remote areas to facilitate access to the approximately 240 remote villages and communities before the spring breakup.

The 2020 Census is a complex organization of people and systems that need to work together to ensure that we are able to count every person living in the Country. The Census Bureau relies on its invaluable partnership with the American Indian and Alaska Native communities to help guide us in our task.

I look forward to continued partnership with you and our tribal partners as we approach 2020. Thank you for the opportunity to be here today, and I look forward to your questions.

[The prepared statement of Mr. Jarmin follows:]

PREPARED STATEMENT OF RON S. JARMIN, ASSOCIATE DIRECTOR FOR ECONOMIC PROGRAMS, PERFORMING THE NON-EXCLUSIVE FUNCTIONS AND DUTIES OF THE DIRECTOR, U.S. CENSUS BUREAU

Good morning Chairman Hoeven, Vice Chairman Udall, and Members of the Committee. I welcome the opportunity to talk with you today about the Census Bureau's work to ensure a high quality enumeration of the American Indian and Alaska Native communities in the 2020 Census. I am excited to have the opportunity to discuss our ongoing government-to-government relationships with American Indian and Alaska Native tribes. We have worked together to plan a 2020 Census that will count everyone on tribal lands once, only once, and in the right place.

While the Census Bureau is planning the most automated, and modern, decennial census in history, we have not disregarded, and in fact recognize more than ever, the unique challenges associated with conducting the decennial census in American Indian and Alaska Native areas. We share the concerns that tribal delegates have raised about the undercount of American Indians and Alaska Natives in previous counts, and are committed to improving this in the 2020 Census.

The 2018 End-to-End Census Test, which is our last opportunity to validate our design and readiness for the 2020 Census, is now underway and field operations will continue through the summer. Following the test, we will finalize plans for all operations and make any necessary adjustments to ensure readiness for the 2020 Census enumeration, which will kick off in remote Alaskan villages on January 20, 2020.

Tribal Engagement

To help us prepare for the 2020 Census, we have continued to build and implement our tribal partnership and we have received vital insights and advice from our tribal partners. We held a series of invaluable consultations with tribal leaders from across the nation, we meet monthly with tribal representatives, and we have continued our ongoing engagements with the Census Bureau's National Advisory Committee on Racial, Ethnic and Other Populations (NAC). The NAC has included several distinguished representatives of the Nation's tribal communities, including my fellow witnesses and trusted Census Bureau partners.

For the 2020 Census, we began consultations with tribal representatives in 2015, two years earlier in the census lifecycle than in prior censuses. The Census Bureau held 17 tribal consultations and one national webinar with federally- and state-recognized tribes and Alaska regional and village corporations. We met with over 400 tribal delegates representing over 250 different tribes, corporations, and organizations.

What We Have Heard. . .

On Enumeration—The Census Bureau informed the tribes that the 2020 Census would have four response options: Internet, telephone, paper, and enumerator. Some tribes reported that Internet response is currently not a viable option for many tribal citizens and requested an in-person enumerator. The Census Bureau is aware Internet access is an issue in rural areas and therefore plans to include a paper questionnaire in the first 2020 Census mailing to households in these areas. As well, the Census Bureau will provide all households—regardless how remote or urban—the option of respond via telephone.

On Partnerships—Tribal delegates shared with us their interest in effective communication between their tribal representatives and the staff working on the 2020 Census in the field. Their focus was on ensuring the Census Bureau provides clear guidance and training to the Census Bureau field offices such as recognizing the unique preferences and challenges among the diverse tribal communities to ensure the most effective engagement with each tribe.

On Population Statistics—The Census Bureau discussed with tribes how the American Indian and Alaska Native responses from the race question were coded, classified, and tabulated under each federally recognized, state-recognized or non-recognized tribe names. A tribal classification code list was presented to the tribes for review and input for any name changes or additions. While this list was presented to tribal leadership during the consultations, the Census Bureau will continue the government-to-government relationship by formally soliciting feedback on the coding and classification of their tribal responses. The formal letter, along with the coding list, will be sent to tribal leadership in spring of 2018.

On Tribal Enrollment—A large majority of the tribes were not in favor of a tribal enrollment question. Tribes expressed that the self-response option will not allow us to collect accurate data, given the differences and complexity of tribal enrollment across American Indian and Alaska Native populations. Tribal enrollment is private information, and the inquiry would infringe upon tribal sovereignty. Tribes also expressed that the Federal Government does not need to collect tribal enrollment data.

This valuable input is a good example of how our tribal engagements are successful. Based on these types of consultations, the Census Bureau made the decision not to include a tribal enrollment question on the 2020 Census or on the American Community Survey.

Actions Underway for the 2020 Census

I would like to now share the concrete plans we have underway, and how each has been tailored to maximize our ability to count the American Indian and Alaska Native communities.

Continuing with our Partnerships

The Census Bureau has had an American Indian and Alaska Native Partnership Program since 2000, and we continue to meet with our regional tribal partnership staff each month to share the most current information about Census Bureau processes as well as to elicit information on best practices from tribal partners. This program has been instrumental in spearheading programs such as the Tribal Complete Count Committees, which have documented successful census outreach efforts on tribal lands. To date, more than 50 tribes and representative tribal associations have appointed a 2020 Census Tribal Liaison to work with our regional tribal partnership staff to prepare for the census. These tribal liaisons will help the Census Bureau in many ways—from developing effective census materials, to finding efficient ways to recruit and hire tribal citizens to manage and conduct field operations, to encouraging tribal response to ensure the most accurate counts.

Creating an Effective Communication Plan

The Census Bureau is planning a robust Integrated Partnership and Communications program—a critical component of the effort to reach and motivate individuals in all areas of the country. Our National Partnership Program will be ramping up beginning in October 2018, and we plan to increase the number of partnership specialists who form these critical relationships in communities across the country from fewer than 800 in the 2010 Census to 1,000 specialists for the 2020 Census.

Leveraging highly localized outreach campaigns, we plan to develop customized marketing and communications materials that can be downloaded and printed for use by our American Indian and Alaska Native partners. We will be assisted in this task by our g&g Advertising, a nationally recognized leader in tailored outreach to American Indians and Native Alaskan audiences and a veteran of two previous decennial census advertising programs. Together, we will be working with our tribal community partners to develop effective outreach materials.

Ensuring Up-to-Date Geographic Information

The Census Bureau has long engaged tribal governments to ensure the accuracy of tribal addresses, streets, and boundaries. This work is critical for the accurate collection, tabulation, and dissemination of census data.

In 2014, the Census Bureau and the National American Indian Housing Council (NAIHC) signed a Memorandum of Understanding establishing a joint statistical project. Then in 2016, the Census Bureau and Bureau of Indian Affairs signed a Memorandum of Understanding to improve the dissemination of accurate data, in furtherance of the government-to-government relationship between the United States and Indian tribes. This Memorandum of Understanding facilitates the sharing of geographic information and databases.

Each year, the Census Bureau conducts the Boundary and Annexation Survey (BAS). The BAS is the only survey to collect legal boundaries from federal recognized tribes, local, county and state governments ensuring that their legal boundaries are current and accurate. Consequently, the official population counts within those boundaries are correctly recorded with the Federal Government. Every year, tribal governments use the BAS to update their federal reservation and off-reservation trust land boundaries. In the most recent 2017 BAS, we received responses from 47.0 percent of tribal governments, up slightly from 44.5 percent and 42.5 percent in 2016 and 2015, respectively. In 2018, we will be adding staff to conduct nonresponse follow-up which we hope will further increase these response rates.

Before every census, we offer representatives from tribal, state, and local governments the opportunity to participate in the Local Update of Census Addresses program. Through this program, governments are able to review and comment on the Census Bureau's residential address list for their jurisdiction. This program is critical for the Census Bureau as we rely on a complete and accurate address list to reach all living quarters and associated population for inclusion in the census. To date, more than 130 tribal governments have registered to review and update the Census Bureau's address list and maps as part of the Local Update of Census Addresses in preparation for the 2020 Census.

Developing Adaptive Modes for Self Response

For the first time, the 2020 Census will provide residents multiple modes for responding to the census in order to maximize self-response. So, while one option will be the Internet, individuals also have the option to respond by telephone through our Census Questionnaire Assistance call centers or through paper questionnaire (which will be mailed as a final attempt before sending enumerators into neighborhoods). In areas where American Community Survey and Federal Communications Commission data show low Internet access, we will be including a paper questionnaire in the first Census 2020 mailing. In some areas where postal mail might not be an effective option for reaching the population, we will be delivering the questionnaire to households personally. At the same time, we will collect any address information we can to facilitate future options for communication with the household.

After giving the population an opportunity to self-respond, we will send enumerators to visit every non-responding household in every location throughout the country (with the exception of remote areas of Alaska where there will already be a full in-person enumeration, as described next). If the enumerator is unsuccessful at making contact with a member of the household after numerous visits, they will attempt to interview a nearby neighbor who could provide proxy information about the household. The intent is to obtain, at a minimum, an accurate population count for each non-responding household during this operation.

Enumerating Remote Areas of Alaska

Alaska's vast, sparsely settled areas traditionally are the first to be counted starting in January of the census year. Local census takers must start enumerating in the approximately 240 remote villages and communities while the frozen ground allows limited access. Many residents leave after the spring thaw to fish and hunt or for other warm-weather jobs, making it difficult to get an accurate count on April 1 "Census Day."

Remote Alaska enumeration has unique challenges associated with accessibility to communities in Alaska's most isolated areas, where population ranges from a few people to several hundred people. Communities are widely scattered and rarely linked by roads. For these communities, we must rely on unique modes of transportation including small planes, snowmobiles, and dogsleds. Because of the logistical challenges, we combine operations for address canvassing and enumeration into one operation called Update Enumerate. During this operation, field staff will update the address lists and maps for the villages and communities, and then conduct an in-person interview at all living quarters to complete the census questionnaire. This will be done at all housing units, group quarters, and transitory locations. We will work with our local partners to be sure all living quarters are enumerated. Outreach to begin preparing for these operations will begin next year in 2019.

Learning through Field Tests

The 2018 End-to-End Census Test began in August 2017 in Pierce County, Washington; Providence County, Rhode Island; and the Bluefield-Beckley-Oak Hill, West Virginia area with the implementation of an address canvassing operation. The in-field portion of the test will continue through August 2018 in Providence County, Rhode Island with the implementation of "peak operations" that include Internet self-response and non-response follow-up. In the address canvassing portions of the test, we had the opportunity to test all of our applications and systems and hone the address list development operations in a wide range of geographical situations, including mountainous areas and areas with low connectivity (Internet and cellular). The lessons we learned from this portion of the test will be particularly useful as we start to prepare for listing in the more remote and rural portions of the country. As the peak operations portion of the 2018 End-to-End Census Test begin in the spring, we look forward to understanding how our enumeration applications and systems function in areas with low connectivity in preparation for the challenges we will surely face when conducting the 2020 Census.

Conclusion

The 2020 Census is a complex organization of people and systems that work together to ensure that we are able to count every person living in the U.S. The Census Bureau relies on its invaluable partnership with the American Indian and Alaska Native communities to help guide us in our task. Through this partnership, we have received valuable advice we believe has made the 2020 Census stronger than ever before in its ability to connect with and represent the American Indian and Alaska Native communities.

The CHAIRMAN. Thank you, Mr. Jarmin.

Ms. GORE.

STATEMENT OF CAROL GORE, PRESIDENT/CEO, COOK INLET HOUSING AUTHORITY

Ms. GORE. Thank you. [Phrase in Native language.] Good afternoon, Chairman Hoeven, Vice Chairman Udall, Alaska Senator Murkowski, and distinguished members of the Senate Committee on Indian Affairs. Thank you for the opportunity to appear today.

My name is Carol Gore. I am a proud Alaskan of Aleut descent and I have been with Cook Inlet Housing for more than 17 years as the President and CEO. Cook Inlet Housing is a tribally-designated housing entity for Cook Inlet region in Alaska. I have also served as the Vice Chair of the Census Bureau's National Advisory Committee since 2014.

The Census Bureau's work impacts Tribes in many ways. It promotes our fair and equal participation in American democracy, provides equal data for research and planning purposes, enables the enforcement of Federal nondiscrimination laws, and draws fair allocations of funding for the Federal programs that are vital to Native communities, including housing, health care, and education.

For decades, Native communities have been undercounted. This is largely because so many Native people live in what the Census Bureau calls hard-to-count communities, which are characterized by their cultural and language barriers, high levels of poverty, unemployment, housing insecurity, lack of telephone and internet access, and remoteness. Collectively, the States represented by the members of this Committee are home to over 900,000 Native people living in hard-to-count communities.

Accurately counting these Native people requires additional resources. Unfortunately, appropriators have restricted the Census Bureau's funding in recent years, directing that the 2020 Census should cost no more than the 2010 Census did. This mandate ignores declining purchasing power due to inflation, the need to count 30 million more Americans, and the increasing complexity of ensuring data security and confidentiality.

Funding shortfalls have already harmed Indian Country. The Bureau planned to test immigration procedures on the Standing Rock and Colville Reservations in 2017. Those tests were cancelled due to a lack of funding. Without testing, the Bureau will be forced to use unproven methods in Indian Country in 2020.

Insufficient funding has also damaged the Bureau's ability to engage with Tribes through its partnership program which conducts targeted outreach to Native and non-Native communities throughout the U.S. In 2010, the Bureau employed 3,800 partnership staff during peak operations. Shockingly, the Bureau has so far been able to hire just 43 partnership specialists.

Back home in Alaska, a single partnership specialist conducts all the Bureau's outreach to the 229 Tribes in our State. She is also responsible for the Bureau's outreach to every municipality, city, bureau, and other unit of local government across our State. As if that charge were not absurd enough, our partnership specialist does not just cover Alaska; she is also responsible for a four-State region. This is clearly an impossible task.

To ensure that the 2020 Census does not undercount Native persons, appropriators must fund the Census Bureau at a reasonable level. By investing in the Bureau's testing efforts, partnership program, and communications campaign, Congress can ensure a more accurate count in Indian Country and save taxpayers money by reducing the need for expensive non-response follow-up.

Census Bureau leadership will also influence the success or failure of the 2020 Census in accurately counting Native people. The immediate past director was willing to listen to tribal perspectives and carefully reflected upon the information we provided before making decisions that affected our people. Currently, the position of the census director is vacant. The person chosen to lead the Census Bureau will greatly influence the future of Indian Country, and I ask for your help to ensure that the role is filled by a principled, bipartisan individual with relevant professional expertise and a strong desire to work with Indian Country.

While the focus of the hearing is the 2020 Decennial Census, I am compelled to also stress the importance of the Census Bureau's Annual American Community Survey. The ACS is the best available resource of uniform data in Indian Country across the Nation.

It remains critical to Indian Country that Congress adequately fund the ACS and that ACS response remain mandatory.

Finally, I would like to recognize the talented, dedicated employees of the Census Bureau for their authentic engagement on tribal issues. I have had the pleasure to work with many of them, and I am here today to tell you that the incredible people at the Census Bureau are not the reason I fear that Native people will be undercounted in 2020. I fear we will be undercounted because there are too few of them and because they are not being given the resources they need to do their jobs properly. I ask you today to help change that.

Thank you for the opportunity, and I look forward to your questions.

[The prepared statement of Ms. Gore follows:]

PREPARED STATEMENT OF CAROL GORE, PRESIDENT/CEO, COOK INLET HOUSING AUTHORITY

Good afternoon Chairman Hoeven, Vice-Chairman Udall, Senator Murkowski, and distinguished members of the Senate Committee on Indian Affairs. Thank you for the opportunity to appear today as the Committee discusses counting all of Indian Country in the 2020 Decennial Census.

My name is Carol Gore. I am a proud Alaskan of Aleut descent. For more than seventeen years, I have served as the President and CEO of Cook Inlet Housing Authority, the Tribally Designated Housing Entity for Alaska's Cook Inlet Region. Since 2014, I have also served as the Vice-Chair of the National Advisory Committee of the U.S. Census Bureau.

As an Alaska Native, a member of the National Advisory Committee, and the President of a Native organization that relies heavily upon Census data, I understand firsthand the importance of an accurate Census count in 2020, especially when it comes to counting Native populations. My statement today is intended to help explain how Census data impacts Indian Country, why it is so difficult to accurately count Native populations, and how Congress and the U.S. Census Bureau can ensure an accurate count of all Native people in 2020 and beyond.

Census Data Matter to Indian Country

The work done by the Census Bureau impacts tribes in a variety of ways. It promotes their fair representation in our democracy, provides data that are used for research and planning purposes, enables government agencies to enforce federal nondiscrimination laws, and drives fair and equitable allocations of federal funding.

The Democratic Process

Census data determine state and local legislative boundaries and the apportionment of seats in the U.S. House of Representatives. The ability of Native people to participate equally in our democracy depends upon the fairness of redistricting processes at the federal, state, and local levels. Those processes, in turn, rest on the accuracy of Census Bureau data. When Native peoples are undercounted, they are denied a full voice in policy decisionmaking and the needs of tribal communities may not be prioritized according to their true proportion of the population.

Research and Planning

Census data are vital for tribal planning purposes. Tribes and tribal organizations rely on accurate Census data to make informed decisions for the futures of their people, including identifying housing and healthcare needs and determining the most appropriate strategies to deploy scarce resources to meet those needs. Tribal businesses utilize Census data to make decisions about their workforce and to measure the risk of capital investments.

Enforcement of Federal Non-Discrimination Laws

For historically marginalized populations like Alaska Natives and American Indians, Census data also serve the function of ensuring that federal civil rights and voting rights laws are properly enforced. Census data are also used to ensure that financial institutions comply with federally-imposed obligations to serve minority populations, including Native Americans.

Equitable Allocation of Federal Funding

Census data play a central role in the determining how federal resources are allocated to tribes and tribal organizations. Following are some of the numerous programs that impact Native communities and are funded, in whole or in part, based upon Census data:

- *Title I Grants to Local Education Agencies*—Provides financial assistance to local educational agencies and schools with high numbers or percentages of low-income children. About 90 percent of Native students attend Title I public schools. [1]
- *Head Start Program*—Provides grants to local agencies to provide child development services to economically disadvantaged children and families, with a special focus on helping preschoolers develop early reading and math skills. Approximately 10 percent of Native children and pregnant women participated in Head Start or Early Head Start during the 2015–16 school year. [2]
- *Native American Employment and Training*—Provides Native peoples with employment training and skills, as well as support for daycare and transportation services to enable Native peoples to thrive in the workplace. There were 313 grant recipients in Native communities in 2013.
- *Indian Health Service*—Provides access to comprehensive and culturally acceptable healthcare to Native people, a critical program to fulfill the federal treaty and trust obligations to tribal people. IHS serves 2.2 million Native people nationwide [3] and uses Census data for planning and program implementation. [4]
- *Medicaid*—In 2015, 42.8 percent of American Indians and Alaska Natives were enrolled in Medicaid or some other public insurance program. [5] Medicaid also provides critical supplemental revenue for the chronically under-funded IHS. [6]
- *Urban Indian Health Program*—Reaches Native people who are not able to access the hospitals, health care centers, or contract health services managed by the IHS and tribal health programs. Approximately 25 percent of Native peoples live in urban areas located in counties served by these programs. [7]
- *Supplemental Nutrition Assistance Program*—The most important tool to prevent hunger and malnutrition among families in the U.S. More than one-fourth of Native households nationally and 31.8 percent on reservations received SNAP benefits in 2015. [8]
- *Special Programs for the Aging* (Title VI, Part A)—Provides grants to Tribal organizations that deliver home and community-based services to Native elders.
- *Indian Housing Block Grant*—Funded the construction or rehabilitation of more than 5,000 homes in 2015. [9] The Census data used to determine IHBG allocations are also used to allocate funding for the Tribal Transportation Programs administered by the Bureau of Indian Affairs.
- *Indian Community Development Block Grants*—Assists low-to-moderate income tribal communities to improve housing conditions, develop community resources, and promote economic development.

Census data are central to ensuring that tribes receive fair allocations of funding for vital federal programs. In fact, when American Indian and Alaska Native (AIAN)

---

[1] "Table: Children in Title I Schools by Race and Ethnicity." Kids Count Data Center, Retrieved 13 December 2017.

[2] "Factsheet: Will You Count? American Indians and Alaska Natives in the 2020 Census." Georgetown Law Center on Poverty and Inequality and the Leadership Conference Education Fund, Updated January 15, 2018 (Citing Data from "Head Start Program Facts Fiscal Year 2016," Early Childhood Learning & Knowledge Center, June 2017).

[3] "IHS 2016 Profile." Indian Health Service, April 2017.

[4] "Trends in Indian Health: 2014 Edition." Indian Health Service, March 2015.

[5] "Policy Basics: Introduction to Medicaid." Center on Budget and Policy Priorities, 16 August 2016.

[6] "Indian Health and Medicaid." Medicaid, Retrieved 13 December 2017; "Health Care: Implementing Our Values in the Federal Health Care Budget." National Congress of American Indians, Retrieved 13 December 2017.

[7] "Urban Health Program Fact Sheet." Indian Health Service, U.S. Department of Health and Human Services, October 2015.

[8] "Table B22005C: Selected Population Profile in the United States: 2015 American Community Survey 1–Year Estimates." U.S. Census Bureau, 2015; "Receipt of Food Stamps/SNAP in the Past 12 Months by Race of Householder (American Indian/Alaska Native Alone)". U.S. Census Bureau, Retrieved 13 December 2017.

[9] "PIH Native American Housing Block Grants." U.S. Department of Housing and Urban Development, Retrieved 13 December 2017. Available at *https://archives.hud.gov/news/2015/pr15-013-14-FY16CJ-NAHBGRANTS.pdf.*

populations are undercounted, states with higher AIAN populations, the very States represented by the members of this Committee, receive less than their fair share of federal resources.

The Difficulty of Accurately Counting Native Populations

Counting the AIAN population accurately, in Alaska and throughout Indian Country, is no simple task. Native communities have been undercounted for decades.[10] The Census Bureau's coverage measurement evaluation for the 2010 Decennial Census show that an estimated 4.9 percent of the AI/AN on-reservation AIAN population was undercounted.[11] The undercount of the AIAN population was potentially higher in parts of my home state, Alaska, where the Census Bureau estimated an 8 percent undercount of what it calls "special-enumeration tracts"—the very places with the highest percentage of Alaska Native people.

2010 Census undercounted American Indian/Alaska Natives by 4.9 percent

American Indian and Alaska Natives—-4.9 percent
Black—-2.1
Hispanic—-1.5
Native Hawaiian and Other Pacific Islander—-1.3
Asian—-0.1
Non-Hispanic white—0.8

The historical undercount of AIAN persons has occurred largely because so many Alaska Native and American Indian people live in what the Census Bureau calls "hard-to-count" geographies. Hard-to-count geographies are characterized by high levels of poverty and unemployment, housing insecurity and homelessness, households lacking telephone and Internet access, households with young children, and lower than average rates of educational attainment. These tracts require special outreach, additional resources, and specific enumeration methods to ensure an accurate count.

The states represented by members of this committee are home to over 900,000 American Indians and Alaska Natives living in hard-to-count Census tracts. Nationally, more than 30 percent of the AIAN population lives in hard-to-count areas.[12] In Alaska, this number jumps to over 65 percent, and in New Mexico, nearly four out of five of American Indians live in hard-to-count communities.[13]

What makes the AIAN population so difficult to count? Geography plays a significant role. American Indians and Alaska Natives disproportionately live in rural environments that are harder for the Census Bureau to reach. This is true in my home state of Alaska, where homes in many Alaska Native Villages do not have traditional mailing addresses and where door-to-door counting requires Census enumerators to take small "bush" planes to and from extremely remote areas of the state.

The manner in which homelessness manifests in Native communities also contributes to the difficulty of obtaining an accurate count. In 2017, the Department of Housing and Urban Development released its Assessment of American Indian, Alaska Native, and Native Hawaiian Housing Needs. HUD recognized that incidents of literal homelessness are rare in many Native communities because of a cultural inclination to take in friends and family members who have no other housing options, even when the result is extreme overcrowding. HUD found that there are up to 85,000 homeless Native Americans living in tribal areas. These individuals lack a permanent, traditional mailing address and are at significant risk of going uncounted in the Decennial Census.

In 2020, the Census Bureau will, for the first time, offer people the option to complete the Decennial Census online. States from New Mexico to Montana to North Dakota are home to remote Census tracts where less than 60 percent of households met the FCC's minimum threshold of Internet connectivity in 2016. Like disproportionate rates of homelessness, limited Internet connectivity could threaten the Census Bureau's ability to accurately count Indian Country in 2020, particularly if the

---

[10] Brownrigg, Leslie and Manuel de la Puente. "Sociocultural Behaviors Correlated with Census Undercount." Paper prepared for presentation in Special Session 2 15 to the American Sociological Association, 22 August 2003.

[11] US Census Bureau, American Community Survey, 5-year Estimates for 2012–2016.

[12] "TABLE 1b: States Ranked by Percent of American Indian/Alaska Natives (race alone or in combination) living in Hard-to-Count (HTC) Census Tracts." The Leadership Conference Education Fund, Retrieved 9 February 2018. Available at *http://civilrightsdocs.info/pdf/census/ 2020/Table1b-States-Percent-AIAN-HTC.pdf.*

[13] "TABLE 1b: States Ranked by Percent of American Indian/Alaska Natives (race alone or in combination) living in Hard-to-Count (HTC) Census Tracts." The Leadership Conference Education Fund, Retrieved 9 February 2018. Available at *http://civilrightsdocs.info/pdf/census/ 2020/Table1b-States-Percent-AIAN-HTC.pdf.*

Bureau lacks the resources necessary to test the efficacy of Internet response in communities with sizeable AIAN populations. While we believe it is critical for the Bureau to carefully plan and test the use of Internet response in Indian Country, we must note, regrettably, that delayed and insufficient funding for the Census Bureau in Fiscal Years 2017 and 2018 forced the Census Bureau to cancel all planned tests of census operations in Indian Country and rural areas—a concern discussed later in my testimony.

Cultural differences also present a challenge for the Bureau when it counts AIAN populations. Native communities have unique customs, and in many, English is not the primary language spoken. Without proper education and training, enumerators may have difficulty communicating effectively with people living in some Native communities. We must also acknowledge that many American Indian and Alaska Native households remain deeply distrustful of the federal government due to historical trauma, which can impact their willingness to cooperate with the Bureau's enumeration efforts.

The 2020 Decennial Census will be unlike any Census ever conducted in the United States. It will rely largely on households responding online, rather than by submitting a paper questionnaire. It will require a large and complex system of computer hardware and software, which has encountered serious problems during development. Outreach and communications efforts, which are of critical importance to Indian Country, are likely to be scaled back due to funding shortfalls. In my home state of Alaska, where 92,000 Native people live in hard-to-count communities, we are extremely concerned about the potential for a significant undercount of the AIAN population during the next Decennial Census. However, it is not too late for Congress to influence a better and more equitable outcome for Indian Country in 2020.

Promoting an Accurate Count of American Indian and Alaska Native People

What can Congress and the Census Bureau do to ensure an accurate count of Indian Country in 2020? While there are certain revenue-neutral measures that Congress and the Administration can take, including appointing qualified, professional, and nonpartisan leadership to oversee Census Bureau operations, the reality is that conducting a fair and accurate Census will require additional resources.

Census Bureau Funding

Appropriators have significantly restricted the Census Bureau's funding in recent years, directing that the 2020 Census should cost no more than the 2010 Census did. [14] This mandate was issued despite the decline in purchasing power due to inflation, the need to count approximately 30 million more Americans, and the increasing complexity of ensuring the security and confidentiality of the data collected.

The significance of recent Census Bureau funding shortfalls is illustrated in the graph below, which compares the funding trend for the upcoming 2020 Decennial Census to the funding trends for the three previous decennial censuses. As the graph shows, Census Bureau funding usually ramps up in the few years preceding the decennial census, but this has not been the case so far for the 2020 Decennial.

---

[14] U.S. Senate, Committee on Appropriations, "Report on Departments of Commerce and Justice, and Science, and Related Agencies Appropriations Bill, 2015," June 5, 2014, Page 20.

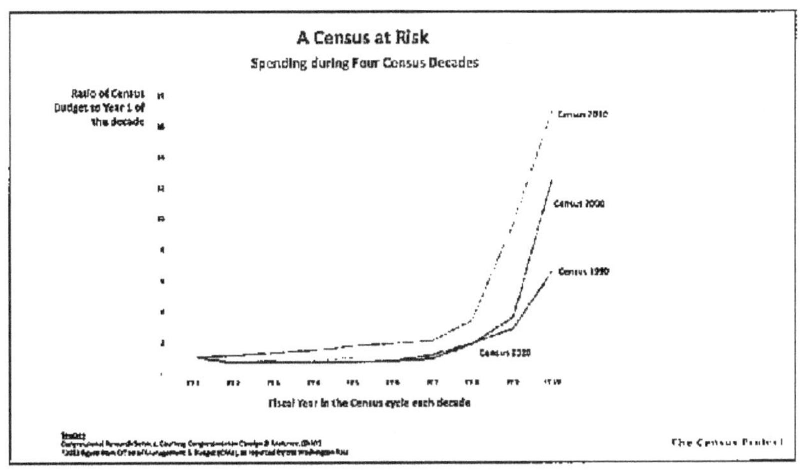

Census Bureau funding shortfalls have already significantly impacted Indian Country. Prior to each of the last several decennials, the Bureau tested its enumeration procedures in reservation areas. Tests were planned for April 2017 on the Standing Rock reservation in North and South Dakota and the Colville reservation in north-central Washington. These tests were intended to refine the Bureau's methods for enumerating areas with unique location characteristics, where it could not mail a Census form to a street address. The tests were also intended to evaluate the integration of Census Bureau systems for the specific type of enumeration most frequently used in remote and rural tribal communities. [15]

The Census Bureau abruptly cancelled the tests on the Standing Rock and Coleville Reservations in October of 2016. The Bureau memo describing the cancellation stated:

> "The proposed funding levels in both the House and Senate from the spring of 2016 require us to prioritize other activities in 2017 rather than expend the resources necessary to conduct two planned 2020 Census field tests in 2017. Given the current uncertainty about 2017 funding, the Census Bureau will not continue expending resources to prepare for the FY 2017 field tests, only to receive insufficient resources to conduct them." [16]

Underfunding of Census Bureau operations indisputably caused the cancellation of testing on the Standing Rock and Coleville Reservations. An insufficient budget request for the Census Bureau in FY 2018 also caused the cancellation of two of three planned "dress rehearsal" sites in 2018. The Census Bureau originally planned to conduct the 2018 End-to-End Census Test for Providence County, Rhode Island; Pierce County, Washington; and the Bluefield-Beckley-Oak Hill area of West Virginia. Testing was cancelled for all sites except Providence County, leaving the Bureau without any experience as to how the Census process may work in 2020 in rural areas, on reservations, and in many other tribal communities. Without testing, the Bureau will be forced to use unproven methods and operations in Indian Country in 2020. That's like flying a prototype airliner for the first time with a full complement of 300 passengers on board. It is imperative that Congress fund additional focused testing in 2018 or 2019 to compensate for the canceled tests on reservations and in rural areas.

Insufficient funding has also damaged the Bureau's ability to engage with tribes and tribal organizations through its Partnership Program. Obtaining an accurate count in Native communities requires significant outreach efforts that individually target each tribal community, engaging persons and organizations the local community trusts and vigorously promoting participation in the Decennial Census. The Census Bureau undertakes this crucial work through its Partnership Program.

---

[15] U.S. Census Bureau, "2017 Census Test; Preparing for the 2020 Census, Colville Indian Reservation and Off-Reservation Trust Land, WA," undated.

[16] U.S. Census Bureau, 2020 Census Program Memorandum Series, "Adjustment of FY 2017 Test Scope," by Lisa M. Blumerman dated October 18, 2016.

In 2010, the Census Bureau employed approximately 3,800 partnership staff during peak operations. By comparison, the Bureau plans to hire just 800 Partnership Specialists for the 2020 Census, according to congressional testimony provided by Commerce Secretary Ross last October. Even more concerning is the fact that the Bureau has hired only 43 Partnership Specialists to date. Back home in Alaska, a single Partnership Specialist conducts the Bureau's outreach to all 229 federally recognized tribes in our state. Our Partnership Specialist must also handle all of the Bureau's outreach efforts with each and every municipality, city, borough, and other unit of local government across Alaska. As if that charge were not unreasonable enough, our Partnership Specialist does not just cover Alaska; she is expected to serve a four-state region. It is an impossible task.

Forty-three Partnership Specialists nationwide would be an entirely insufficient number to engage trusted community members and mobilize local education and outreach efforts in Indian Country alone. Expecting those few dozen people to complete that work for every single community throughout United States of America is patently absurd. We call upon Congress to provide sufficient funding for the Bureau to immediately hire another 157 Partnership Specialists, bringing the total number of Partnership Specialists to 200 in 2018, just 5.3 percent of the number hired for the 2010 Decennial Census. Further, we urge Congress to provide funding for roughly 2,000 Partnership Specialists and assistants during peak preparations and operations in 2019 and 2020. Given the growing challenges to a fair and accurate 2020 Census, a greater outreach effort will help overcome fear and distrust of the federal government in Native communities and help keep overall census costs in check.

Like its Partnership Program, the Bureau's communications campaign is a vital investment to ensure a cost-effective and accurate census. The Commerce Department recently concluded that public cooperation in 2020 will be lower than originally projected, which will increase costs substantially. A robust advertising and outreach campaign could help ease public concerns cyber-security, confidentiality, and the safety of responding to the Census. It is also critical to determine the targeted messaging that will be most effective in specific hard-to-count communities, like those throughout Indian Country. Unfortunately, campaign planning, messaging research, and testing is already many months behind schedule because of insufficient funding. Congress should provide increased funding in FY 2018–2020 to put the Bureau's communications campaign back on track.

Underfunding the Bureau's Partnership Program and communications campaign is penny wise and pound foolish. The Census Bureau has estimated that its costs increased by approximately $85 million for each one percent of households that did not mail back their census form in 2010. A reasonably staffed Partnership Program and an effective communications campaign can significantly reduce the rate of non-responding households, making them sound investments in an accurate and cost-efficient census.

To ensure that the 2020 Decennial Census does not exacerbate the undercount of American Indian and Alaska Native persons that occurred in 2010, appropriators should fund the Census Bureau's Periodic Censuses and Programs budget at $1.578 billion for 2018, for a total Census Budget of $1.848 billion. This figure includes the administration's adjusted budget request (+$187 million more than its original budget proposal), plus $164 million more to expand the partnership and communications programs and to begin to increase the number of local census offices.

Census Bureau Leadership

Leadership of the Census Bureau, particularly at the Director level, will greatly influence the success or failure of the 2020 Decennial Census in accurately counting American Indian and Alaska Native people. The immediate past Director of the Census Bureau demonstrated a willingness to listen to tribal perspectives and the ability to carefully reflect upon the opinions and information provided before making decisions that would affect tribes and AIAN people. He listened alertly during numerous day-long consultation sessions with tribal leaders and representatives of tribal organizations. He also strengthened the role of the Tribal Affairs Coordinator within the Bureau's Office of Congressional and Intergovernmental Affairs.

Currently, the position of Census Bureau Director is vacant. The President has not advanced a nominee, who will be subject to Senate confirmation. Whoever is chosen to lead the Census Bureau will be in a position to greatly influence the future of Indian Country. We ask that the Senate help ensure that the role is filled by a principled individual with relevant professional expertise, substantial management experience, and a willingness to work with the diverse populations impacted by Census Bureau data collections.

Tribal Enrollment Question

The Census Bureau spent considerable time researching and evaluating the risks and potential benefits of including a tribal enrollment question in the 2020 Decennial Census. After careful study and more than a dozen full-day consultation sessions with tribes and tribal organizations from across the country, the Bureau determined that it would not recommend the inclusion of a question on tribal enrollment. I urge the members of this committee to stand by the Bureau's well-informed decision.

It is my understanding that in nearly all of the Bureau's consultation sessions, the significant majority of tribal representatives expressed disapproval of the possible inclusion of a tribal enrollment question. This position was reinforced by the National Congress of American Indians, which passed a resolution explicitly opposing the inclusion of a tribal enrollment question.

Tribes oppose the inclusion of a tribal enrollment question for several reasons. Some tribes have concerns about the implications to tribal sovereignty. Because the Decennial Census is based upon self-identification, the only way for the Bureau to confirm enrollment would involve tribes disclosing their roles for purposes of verification. Tribes were also concerned that the question would produce flawed and inaccurate data. Because there is no universal definition of "tribe" across federal tribal programs, it would be impossible for a single enrollment question to accurately measure "tribal members" for the purposes of federal Native American programs. Additionally, in places like Alaska, many tribal members identify their tribe based upon their racial or ethnic identity. A tribal enrollment question would fail to capture this distinction and would lead to inaccurate data. For these reasons, a tribal enrollment question does not belong on the Decennial Census or any other Census Bureau data collection.

The American Community Survey

While the focus of this hearing is the 2020 Decennial Census, I am compelled to also stress the importance of the Census Bureau's annual American Community Survey (ACS). The ACS is the best available source of uniform data on Native communities across the country. It is utilized in numerous federal funding formulas, including for the Indian Housing Block Grant.

Unlike the Decennial Census, which seeks to count every person in the country, the ACS is a survey. It is sent to a sample of households within any given community. Although the Census Bureau has instituted procedures that increase the sampling rates for American Indian and Alaska Native areas, a measure for which it should be applauded, it remains critical to Indian Country that Congress adequately funds the ACS.

I also urge Congress to ensure that the ACS remains a mandatory data collection. Recent years have seen efforts by some organizations and Members of Congress to make ACS response voluntary. Studies suggest that making the ACS voluntary would lower the national response rate by over 20 percent. To account for this drop in responses the Bureau would need to increase the sample size, which would translate to significantly more federal dollars spent conducting the ACS without any guarantee of improved data reliability or usefulness. In fact, a short-lived "experiment" with a voluntary census form in Canada resulted in the loss of data for about 25 percent of the country's communities, most notably the rural and sparsely populated areas that are home to many of Canada's Native peoples. The Canadian government reversed course when the next census took place, restoring the mandatory response requirement for its survey on household social and economic characteristics.

While there have been limited discussions about creating a new federally-administered tribal survey, the costs of doing so are prohibitive. Various estimates suggest that it would cost between $20 and $140 million to conduct such a survey just once every five years. Considering the substantial unmet needs throughout Indian Country, from health care to housing, we in Alaska prefer to avoid duplicating data collection efforts and instead focus on working with the Census Bureau to enhance the accuracy of the ACS.

Conclusion

I would like to briefly recognize Norm DeWeaver, Terri Ann Lowenthal, and the Leadership Conference on Civil and Human Rights for their distinguished and ongoing work to educate stakeholders across the country about how Census data collections affect Alaska Native and American Indian populations. Their engagement has informed my participation on the Census Bureau's National Advisory Committee and has been deeply appreciated.

I would also like to recognize the talented and dedicated employees of the U.S. Census Bureau for their authentic engagement on tribal issues. I have had the pleasure to work with so many of them over the past half-decade, including Tim Olson, Associate Director for Field Operations, who is deeply passionate about the work the Bureau does. There's James Christy, who heads the Los Angeles Regional Office but now finds himself helping to fill capacity gaps in Bureau Headquarters in Maryland. Jamey has always made time to listen to tribes in Alaska, despite the enormity of his role for the Census Bureau. And of course, there is Dee Alexander, who has brought new accountability to tribes and Native peoples through her role as the Bureau's Tribal Affairs Coordinator. We appreciate and value the work they do every single day.

Please understand that I am here today to tell you that these incredible people and their many colleagues at the Census Bureau are NOT the reason I fear that American Indian and Alaska Native people will be undercounted in 2020. I fear we will be undercounted because there are too few of them and because they are not being given the resources they need to do their jobs thoroughly. I am asking you today, in no uncertain terms, to help change that.

I appreciate the opportunity to appear before the Senate Committee on Indian Affairs, and I hope the information I have provided today has reinforced the vital importance of the 2020 Census for Indian Country.

The CHAIRMAN. Thank you, Ms. Gore.
President Keel.

STATEMENT OF HON. JEFFERSON KEEL, PRESIDENT, NATIONAL CONGRESS OF AMERICAN INDIANS

Mr. KEEL. Thank you, Senator Hoeven, Vice Chairman Udall, and members of the Committee. Before I begin, I want to, first of all, state my support and our support and appreciation for the reauthorization of the Tribal Law and Order Act and improvements to that bill to help secure Indian Country, so thank you for that action. We appreciate that.

On behalf of the National Congress of American Indians, I want to thank you for holding this hearing on how to ensure Indian Country counts in the upcoming decennial census. In the spring of 2020, the Nation will be focused on the decennial census; however, plans and funding are required now for an accurate enumeration, with no differential undercounts.

The upcoming census will be unlike any other census undertaken before. The failure to fully enumerate the American Indian and Alaska Native population could result in devastating consequences, including reductions in access to Federal and State services and resources.

The census is a foundational tenet of American democracy, mandated in the U.S. Constitution and central to America's representative form of government. A fair democracy requires an accurate population count. It is necessary to ensure that Native voters have an equal voice in the political process of non-tribal elections.

As you know, American Indians and Alaska Native people are especially at risk for undercounts. As stated before, the Census Bureau estimates that in the most recent census nearly 5 percent of Native people on reservations were missed. In the 1990 Census, as noted, the net undercount for American Indians on reservations were more than 12 percent.

Some years have been better, though. The undercount was just 1 percent in 2000.

Careful planning and consultation with Tribes and operations in partnerships and adequate resources are critical to addressing the barriers to counting Native people.

A number of factors contribute to Native people being hard to count. The Census Bureau identified the factors that are associated with undercounts in the census. These include poverty, low educational attainment, lacking a telephone, unemployment, and linguistic isolation, among others.

Many of the characteristics that make the Native people at risk for being undercounted persist since 2010, such as economic hardship and low education. In 2015, 38 percent of Native individuals on reservations were living in poverty, compared to 13 percent of the U.S. population.

Young children are also undercounted at high rates, which is concerning given that Native people on reservations have a median age of 9 years lower than the national average.

The Census Bureau will again need the resources for operations counting Native people in the 2020 Census. The credibility of the Census Bureau is critical for public trust and the integrity of the 2020 Census and all census statistics. This is why non-partisan objective census leadership is important. It also makes the partnership program and communications campaign critical to a successful 2020 Census.

Research on barriers and attitudes about the census shows that Native people had the lowest intent to respond in 2010. They also did not believe responding would lead to any positive result in their community. Resources for census partnerships and finding trusted messengers to address Tribal cynicism and suspicion about the use and purpose of the census is critical to a successful 2020 count.

However, as we move into the middle of fiscal year 2018, funding for the Census Bureau is a significant problem. Throughout the entire 2020 Census lifecycle, fiscal year 2012 to 2021, Congress, every year, has not provided the amount of money the Census Bureau requested. This means that the 2020 Census has already been underfunded from the start.

Unfortunately, uncertainty about funding levels resulted in the cancelling of planned field tests on the Standing Rock Reservation in North and South Dakota, and the Colville Reservation in Washington. This eliminated critical testing of methods for the 2020 Census.

In addition to the funding request and strong census leadership, we also oppose the addition of a citizenship question to the 2020 form. Changes to the census form this close to the 2020 Census would jeopardize the response of hard-to-count communities.

We urge the Committee to address the funding and policy concerns raised in this testimony, all issues that are critical to making sure American Indians and Alaska Natives are accurately counted.

Thank you very much.

[The prepared statement of Mr. Keel follows:]

PREPARED STATEMENT OF HON. JEFFERSON KEEL, PRESIDENT, NATIONAL CONGRESS OF AMERICAN INDIANS

On behalf of the National Congress of American Indians (NCAI), I want to thank you for holding this hearing on how to ensure Indian Country counts in the upcoming decennial Census. In the spring of 2020, the attention of the nation will be focused on the decennial Census, however plans and funding are required now for an accurate enumeration, with no differential undercounts. The upcoming Census will be unlike any other census undertaken before. The failure to fully enumerate the American Indian and Alaska Native (AI/AN) population could result in devastating consequences, including reductions in access to federal and state services and resources.

Foundational to Democracy

The Census is a critical and powerful information source that will significantly influence American policy for the coming decade. It is a foundational tenet of American democracy, mandated in article 1, section 2 of the US Constitution and central to our representative form of government. A fair democracy requires an accurate population count.

The U.S. population is enumerated every 10 years and census data are used to allocate Congressional seats, electoral votes, and is the basis for political redistricting. Under the 14th Amendment's guarantee of equal representation, congressional districts must have roughly equal numbers of people, so census data are used to draw district lines. Public Law 94–171 governs the release of census data for redistricting at the federal, state, and local levels, and an accurate count is necessary to ensure that American Indian and Alaska Native voters have an equal voice in the political process of non-tribal elections. Jurisdictions also use census data to comply with the Voting Rights Act, such as making sure Native voters have access to language assistance when they cast their votes in an election.

Essential to Fair Resource Distribution

In addition to its use in fair voting representation, census data play a key role in the fair distribution of billions of dollars to tribes and AI/AN people across the nation. Federal funding for Indian schools, Indian education programs, Indian health programs, Indian housing programs, water and sewage projects, roads, and economic development are distributed on the basis of data collected by the Census Bureau.

American Indians/Alaska Natives at Risk for Undercounts

Certain population groups are at higher risk of being missed in the decennial census—groups considered hard-to-count. Native people especially on reservations and in Alaska Native villages have been historically underrepresented in the census, and in 2020, new methodologies for enumerating the U.S. population could put other groups at risk. In the 2010 Census, the Census Bureau estimates that American Indians and Alaska Natives living on reservations or in Native villages were undercounted by approximately 4.9 percent, more than double the undercount rate of the next closest population group. [1]

The net undercount for American Indians living on reservations was also very high in 1990, with an estimated 12.2 percent missed. About one in three Native people live in hard-to-count census tracts. [2] The Census Bureau identifies twelve characteristics that are associated with census undercounts, including linguistic isolation, poverty, low educational attainment, lacking a telephone, unemployment, and others. [3] A recent report found that although the rural population is generally easier to enumerate than the urban population, certain rural areas will be difficult to count in 2020, such as American Indians on reservations and Alaska Natives, as well as Hispanics in the Southwest, residents of Appalachia, migrant workers, and African Americans in the rural South. [4]

A large proportion of American Indians/Alaska Natives in certain states live in hard-to-count (HTC) tracts; for instance, in New Mexico 78.6 percent of AI/AN people live in HTC tracts, 68.1 percent in Arizona, 65.6 percent in Alaska, 52.4 percent in South Dakota, and 49.9 percent in Montana. [5]

Households in poverty are very hard to count: in 2015, 38.3 percent of Native individuals on reservations were living in poverty compared to the national rate of 13 percent. [6] Young children are also undercounted at disproportionately high rates compared to other age groups, and Native people on reservations have a median age nine years lower than the national average. [7] The poverty rate is 46.3 percent for AI/AN-alone youth ages 0 to 17 in reservation areas. [8] Many of the characteristics that make American Indians and Alaska Native hard to count persist, such as economic hardship and education, and thus the Census Bureau will again need the resources to enumerate accurately the AI/AN population in the 2020 Census.

Barriers, Attitudes, and Motivators

The Census Bureau plans to conduct the Census Barriers, Attitudes, and Motivators Survey (CBAMS) to inform work on the 2020 Census Integrated Partnership and Communications Plan. While attitudes and the political climate may have changed since the 2010 CBAMS, the results of the last study are informative as baseline data to understand the critical need for effective education and outreach activities for 2020. The 2010 CBAMS results showed that among racial and ethnic groups, AI/AN people and Asians had the lowest overall intent to respond. Some of the other relevant findings from then:[9]

- Native people reported less favorability and were less likely to think responding to the Census was important (p. 21).
- AI/ANs felt that they were familiar with the Census and its purpose. However, while AI/ANs understood that the Census "lets government know what my community needs," they did not see results in their community (p. 21).
- They do not tend to consider it a "civic responsibility" to answer the Census, but answering the Census reflects pride in oneself (p. 22).
- Many did not feel it was important to participate in the Census nor did they view it favorable.
- The previous report suggested "that messages targeted to American Indians should focus on appealing to a sense of civic duty as well as on specific information about the Census." (p. 22)
- AI/ANs in particular were characterized by a unique belief profile. They were much more likely than other groups to express skepticism about the use and purposes of the Census and the security of Census data, and they were the only group for which agreement that it is important for everyone to be counted was lower than 90 percent (p. 24).
- American Indians expressed cynicism about the importance of the Census, and they were particularly characterized by suspicion about the use and purpose of the Census (p. 25).

The 2010 report recommended that, "while strong conclusions about this group are not warranted, the data suggest that messages focusing on civic duty might be effective among American Indians" (p. 34). The analysis suggested that while AI/AN people expressed negative feelings about the Census and skepticism, they are relatively knowledgeable about its purpose (p. 36). The report recommended focusing on census as a civic duty, security of census data, and how the Census has benefited AI/AN communities.

These results are important since many aspects of public life have changed since the last Census, with heightened concern around security of digital data, federal government agency breaches, as well as the perception of increasingly strained race relations.

These new elements of the social landscape may exacerbate some of the barriers to Census participation, especially mistrust of government and the perception that participation in the census will lead to improvements in one's community. Messages appealing to civic duty for AI/AN people may also have to be implemented in new ways. However, AI/AN trust in government varies based on whether the government is local (tribal), state, or federal—trust in tribal government is often much higher than trust in the federal government. Finding the trusted messengers in Indian Country is critical to an effective public education and outreach campaign, especially for AI/AN people.

Impacts of Undercounts in Indian Country

Undercounting AI/AN people in the 2020 Census could lead to inefficient distribution of federal funding to tribes. Each tribe and tribal community has unique health, housing, education, and economic development needs. Many programs serving tribes are funded based entirely or in part on census or census-derived data, including the following.

- The *Indian Housing Block Grant Program (IHBG)* is a formula grant that provides a range of affordable housing activities on Indian reservations and Indian areas. The block grant approach to housing for Native Americans was enabled by the Native American Housing Assistance and Self Determination Act of 1996 (NAHASDA). The block grant program, which is based almost entirely on census data, served, helped build, or rehabilitated 5,014 units in 2015.
- Population data used in the IHBG program are also used to allocate money for the *Tribal Transportation Programs* administered by the Bureau of Indian Affairs. Several child welfare programs administered by the Children's Bureau in the Department of Health and Human Services also use Census data for fund allocation.

- The special *Native American workforce programs* under the Workforce Innovation and Opportunity Act distributed almost $49 million for the Comprehensive Services Program and an additional nearly $13 million for the Supplemental Youth Services program in Program Year 2017. The fund allocation system for each of these two programs uses Census data exclusively. The program supports employment and training activities in order to develop more fully the academic, occupational and literacy skills; make individuals more competitive in the workforce; and promote economic and social development in accordance with the goals and values of such communities.
- The *Indian Health Service* provides access to comprehensive and culturally acceptable healthcare to AI/AN people, a critical program that fulfills the federal treaty and trust obligations to tribal people. The IHS provides services to 2.2 million Natives nationwide and uses Census data for planning and implementation of programs. [10] IHS also uses Census data in a number of its funding distribution formulas.

Concerns with the 2020 Census

Careful planning and adequate funding now and leading up to 2020 are essential to minimizing undercounts of the American Indian and Alaska Native population. As we move into the middle of FY 2018, funding for the Census Bureau appears to be a significant problem.

Peak operations for the 2020 Census will start in two years. Early operations are underway for an important "dress rehearsal" in 2018 (the End-to-End Census Test). State, local, and tribal governments are preparing to review address lists and digital maps for their communities (the Local Update of Census Addresses program, or LUCA), which create the universe for the count in 2020. As in every decade, the U.S. Census Bureau must have a steady annual funding ramp-up between now and 2020 for the constitutionally required enumeration, to ensure on-time, comprehensive final testing and preparations.

The Census Bureau is funded through the Commerce, Justice, and Science (CJS) Appropriations bill. Throughout the entire 2020 Census lifecycle (FY 2012–FY 2021), Congress every year has not allocated the amount of money the Census Bureau requested. This means that *the 2020 Census has been underfunded from the start.*

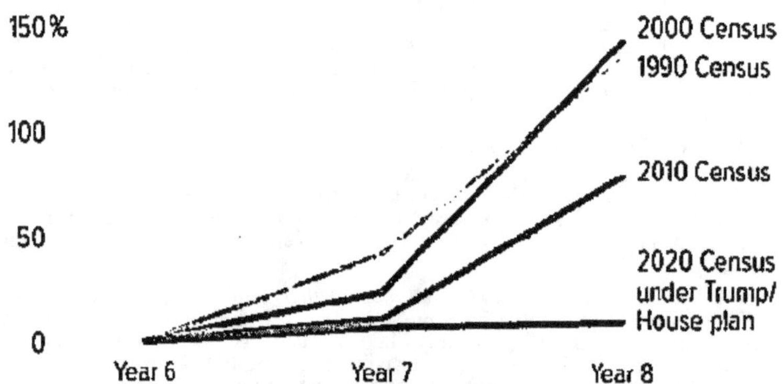

For context, the Census Bureau generally ramps up for the decennial count with a decade-long cycle of spending, starting with research and testing in the fiscal year ending in "2." Generally, after modest but important increases earlier in the decade, Census budgets begin to rise significantly in the fiscal year ending in "6," when the Bureau must begin to operationalize the census design and conduct larger field tests. After preparation during the year ending in "8," address canvassing takes place in the eighth year of the cycle (e.g. 1989 before the 1990 Census).

Census outreach and promotion, as well as recruitment of hundreds of thousands temporary field staff, begins in the year before the census. Peak Census operations start in late January in remote Alaska in the year ending in "0"—Census Year! Census operations wind down in the 10th year of the lifecycle (e.g. 2021), with tabulation and publication of the census data will carry our nation through the next decade.

Impact on American Indians/Alaska Natives

Unfortunately, uncertainty about FY 2017 funding levels and lack of sufficient appropriations resulted in the Census Bureau canceling planned field tests on the Standing Rock Reservation in North and South Dakota and the Colville Reservation and Off-Reservation Trust land in Washington State, which eliminated critical testing of methods for the 2020 Census. These field tests would have helped the Bureau evaluate methods for counting people in tribal areas lacking street addresses, and test methods of making in-person counts in Native households. Inadequate funding has compelled the Census Bureau to announce "pauses" and modifications for key 2020 Census activities, which could greatly diminish the Bureau's ability to take an accurate, cost-effective census and is expected to increase the disproportionate undercount of American Indian and Alaska Natives, especially those living in rural, lowincome, geographically isolated, and/or linguistically isolated households.

Overall Recommendations

NCAI urges Congress to ensure a sufficient funding ramp-up for the 2020 Census in Fiscal Year 2018 and beyond, without undermining other core programs such as the American Community Survey (ACS), Economic Census, and other economic and demographic surveys and programs (such as the Current Population Survey (CPS) and Small Area Health Insurance Estimates (SAHIE), all of which are critical to monitoring the well-being of American Indians and Alaska Natives. NCAI also includes two non-funding recommendations to ensure a successful 2020 Census: urging strong, permanent, and nonpartisan leadership for the Census Bureau and opposing the addition of a citizenship question.

Funding Details

The FY 2018 continuing resolution that runs through March 23, 2018 provides a temporary adjustment of an additional $182 million for the Census Bureau to meet necessary deadlines in preparing for the 2020 Decennial Census. That amount falls short of the Administration's revised FY 2018 funding request of +$187 million over the President's original budget, but it is at least a first step toward full funding. NCAI continues to support the amount needed to fully fund critical outreach, promotion, and partnership activities in the full year appropriations bill for FY 2018.

NCAI urges Congress to enact a total of at least $1.848 billion for the Census Bureau in the *final Omnibus FY 2018 appropriations bill, which Congress must pass and the president must sign by March 23 to avoid another CR or government shutdown.*

NCAI adopted resolution MKE–17–050, "Support for Census Programs, Surveys, and Other Critical Preparations for Accurate Enumeration in the 2020 Census," which calls for full funding for the Census Bureau to meet updated cost projections for the 2020 Census. [11]

Included in the $1.848 billion for the Census Bureau, NCAI supports a total discretionary appropriation of $270 million for *Current Surveys and Programs*, equal to the Senate Appropriations Committee mark and the FY 2017 appropriation.

NCAI also supports a total discretionary appropriation of $1.578 billion for *Periodic Census and Programs,* which is $140 million above the adjusted request for the 2020 Census program. This amount includes:

T32020 Census: $1.127 billion, at a minimum, derived as follows:

- $987 million, administration's adjusted request
- +$50 million for the contingency fund proposed by Commerce Secretary Ross
- +$80 million for development of the communications campaign under Integrated Partnership and Communications contract (Y&R)

- +$10 million to increase the number of Partnership Specialists from 43 to 200 in FY 2018

Further justification:

An increase is needed for communications research and development (+$80 million). NCAI supports additional funding in FY 2018 to expand research and testing (including surveys and focus groups) of effective messaging for the growing number of communities, such as American Indians on reservations and Alaska Natives, at higher risk of undercounting. NCAI considers it critical that the creative development of the advertising campaign is on schedule. The Integrated Partnership and Communications (IPC) contract was awarded a year earlier than the 2010 Census cycle, but budget delays and shortfalls in FY 2017 caused delays in funding the contract for this work. Unfortunately, messaging research and creative development for the advertising campaign are now behind the comparable schedule for the 2010 Census.

NCAI supports restoring some level of testing in rural and remote areas in the next year, which includes methods used on American Indian reservations and in Alaska Native villages. With cancellation of two of three 2018 dress rehearsal sites, the Census Bureau will be forced to use methods and operations in these communities in 2020 that are untested or not fully tested, and which could lead to an undercount and cost increases.

An increase is needed in the number of Partnership Specialists engaged in outreach to state, local, and tribal governments and community-based organizations (+$10 million). Congress should provide increased funding in fiscal years 2018 through 2020 for the Partnership Program and related promotion campaign, which will ensure the 2020 Census is cost-efficient and can help constrain the cost of followup with reluctant, unresponsive households. The Tribal Liaison Program is a very important component of this partnership program in Indian Country and should be funded at no less than it was for the 2010 decennial. Forty-three Partnership Specialists is insufficient to do the outreach and education necessary for the 2020 Census in an increasingly difficult civic environment. The first phase of the 2020 Census communications plan is scheduled to start in a year, and some census offices will open early in 2019 to support preliminary census activities. Tribal officials and tribal 'trusted messengers' at the grassroots level must be prepared to reinforce the Census Bureau's messages, explain census activities, and help identify candidates for temporary census positions. Tribes and tribal organizations will also need to address fears about census participation.

NCAI urges that Congress request a cost estimate for the advance work needed in FY 2018 to increase the number of Area Census Offices to 300 in FY 2019–FY2020 and to include additional funding for this activity in the final FY 2018 Omnibus Appropriations bill. NCAI supports the expansion of the Census Bureau's Areas Census Offices and census takers for peak census operations (2019–2020).

Census Leadership

Census leadership is critical for the agency to carry out its mission of serving as the leading source of objective, quality data about the nation's people and economy. The Census Bureau's leadership must uphold its core principles of protecting confidentiality, sharing expertise, and conducting its work openly and fairly. The Census must be carried out in a non-partisan way, guided by a commitment to objectivity. This person must have an extensive background in demography or the statistical sciences and significant experience in the management of a large public or non-profit organization.

Right now, the need for strong, permanent leadership at the Census Bureau is more important than ever as the agency prepares for the 2020 decennial count. NCAI urges the Administration to put forward candidates for Census Director and Census Bureau Deputy Director who can lead the agency in a nonpartisan, scientifically objective way. A nominee or appointment that undermines the credibility of the Bureau's role as a nonpartisan statistical agency would also imperil the public trust in the integrity of the 2020 Census and all census statistics.

Citizenship Question

In December 2017, the U.S. Department of Justice requested to add a question about citizenship to the 2020 Census. The Constitution requires a count, regardless of citizenship or legal status, of all persons living in the United States on Census Day.

Changes to the census form this close to 2020 Census planning would jeopardize the validity of the tests of alternative questionnaires and designs, which the Census Bureau has spent years testing. A change to the questionnaire now would impact the outreach and partnership strategies designed around different content. Changes to the form would potentially have adverse and unintended consequences for 2020 census operations and the accuracy of the data.

Adding a citizenship question could also have cost implications if added this late in the 2020 Census cycle. The self-response rates that the 2020 Census Operational Plan bases staffing levels on did not include a question on citizenship. Experts expect that adding a question on citizenship will lower initial response, leading to an expanded Nonresponse Follow-up operation, which will increase the cost of the census without improving accuracy. NCAI opposes the Justice Department's request to add a citizenship question to the decennial census.

Conclusion

On behalf of the National Congress of American Indians, we thank you for holding this hearing to ensure Indian Country counts. The decennial census is a foundational tenet of American democracy and central to our representative form of government. A fair democracy requires an accurate population count, including throughout Indian Country. We urge the Committee to address the funding and policy concerns raised in this testimony, all issues that are critical to making sure American Indians and Alaska Natives are accurately counted.

ENDNOTES

1 U.S. Census Bureau. (2012). "Census Bureau Releases Estimates of Undercount and Overcount in the 2010 Census" accessed at *https://www.census.gov/newsroom/releases/archives/2010census/cb12-95.html*

2 Leadership Conference Education Fund. (2018). Table 1a. States Ranked by Number of American Indian/Alaska Natives (race alone or in combination) living in Hard-to-Count (HTC) Census 2 Leadership Conference Education Fund. (2018). Table 1a. States Ranked by T Nraucmtsb. eArc ocef sAsmede raitc an Indian/Alaska Natives (race alone or in combination) living in Hard-to-Count (HTC) Census Tracts. Accessed at *http://civilrightsdocs.info/pdf/census/2020/Table1a-States-Number-AIAN-HTC.pdf*

3 O'Hare, William. (2017). 2020 Census Faces Challenges in Rural America. National Issue Brief #131. University of New Hampshire, Carsey Research

4 O'Hare, William. (2017). 2020 Census Faces Challenges in Rural America. National Issue Brief #131. University of New Hampshire, Carsey Research

5 Leadership Conference Education Fund. (2018). Table 1a. States Ranked by Number of American Indian/Alaska Natives (race alone or in combination) living in Hard-to-Count (HTC) Census Tracts. Accessed at *http://civilrightsdocs.info/pdf/census/2020/Table1a-States-Number-AIAN-HTC.pdf*

6 "Table B17001C: Selected Population Profile in the United States: 2015 American Community Survey 1–Year Estimates." U.S. Census Bureau, Retrieved 13 December 2017. Available at *https://factfinder.census.gov/bkmk/table/1.0/en/ACS/15l1YR/B17001C/0100000US/0100089US.*

7 The Native median age on reservations is 29.1 years compared to the U.S. median age of 37.8 years. "Median Age by Sex (American Indian and Alaska Native)." U.S. Census Bureau, Retrieved 2017. Available at· *https://factfinder.census.gov/bkmk/table/1.0/en/ACS/15l1YR/B01002C/0100000US/0100089US*

8 2012–2016 5-year ACS estimates by land area

9 C2PO 2010 Census Integrated Communications Campaign Research Memoranda Series, No. 11, "Census Barriers, Attitudes and Motivators Survey Analytic Report" May 18, 2009

10 "Trends in Indian Health: 2014 Edition." Indian Health Service, March 2015. Available at *https://www.ihs.gov/dps/publications/trends2014/*

11 MKE–17–050 "Support for Census Programs, Surveys, and Other Critical Preparations for Accurate Enumeration in the 2020 Census" accessed at *http://www.ncai.org/resources/resolutions/support-for-census-programs-surveysand-other-critical-preparations-for-accurate-enumeration-in-the-2020-census*

The CHAIRMAN. Thank you, President Keel.

Mr. TUCKER.

STATEMENT OF JAMES T. TUCKER, PRO BONO VOTING RIGHTS COUNSEL, NATIVE AMERICAN RIGHTS FUND

Mr. TUCKER. Chairman Hoeven, Vice Chairman Udall, and members of the Committee, on behalf of the Native American Rights

Fund, thank you for examining how to make Indian Country count in the 2020 Census.

The 2020 Census is one of the foremost civil rights issues in Indian Country. It serves as the keystone for our representative government. Past undercounts have deprived hundreds of thousands of Native Americans of their voice in government. Without an equal voice in elections, Indian Country is deprived of access to the resources and policy decisions that are so desperately needed in some of the Nation's most economically disadvantaged communities.

In the 2010 Census, the undercount of those living on tribal lands was 4.9 percent, more than double the undercount weight of the next closest population group.

There are significant challenges to making Indian Country count. Historical distrust of the Federal Government often deters responses. One-third of all Native Americans, 1.7 million people, live in hard-to-count census tracts, including geographically isolated rural areas.

Native Americans had the lowest census mail response rate in the 2015 National Content Test, which was exacerbated by lack of traditional mailing addresses and homelessness. Native Americans have the highest poverty rate of any population group, at 26.6 percent. On federally recognized Indian reservations in Alaska Native villages, that rate is 38.3 percent.

Over one quarter of all Native Americans are under 18 years of age, with a third of those below the poverty line. Language barriers and illiteracy are pervasive, especially among thousands of tribal elders in Alaska, Arizona, and New Mexico.

Statistical sampling is more difficult in sparsely populated tribal areas. Most of Indian Country lacks reliable broadband access.

Now, the complexity of factors contributing to the undercount in Indian Country may seem overwhelming, and it is at times, but Census leadership and staff are up to the task. They are impartial, dedicated professionals committed to making sure that every person is counted. But they must be given the tools and resources to do their jobs and make every person count in Indian Country.

The starting point is for fiscal year 2018 appropriations of at least $1.848 billion for the 2020 Census. That funding is needed for the communications campaign, more partnership program specialists, and more area census offices. The planned field tests on the Colville and Standing Rock Reservations must be restored to test enumeration of areas with high concentrations of non-mailable addresses. More resources must be committed to outreach and partnership programs in Indian Country, including program funding to communicate in Native languages.

Outreach coordinators will need to be hired from village and tribal communities to identify, plan, and execute the most effective methods of communicating about the importance of the census and how to ensure an accurate count is obtained.

In addition, the Census 2020 questionnaire should be updated to incorporate the Census Bureau's recommendations from the 2015 NCT, including, number one, providing a write-in line instead of the check boxes for the three American Indian and Alaska Native categories under the very outdated 1997 Federal race and ethnicity standards; number two, giving relevant examples; and, three, offering enough space for multiple responses or to write a longer tribal or village name.

Furthermore, trusted American Indians and Alaska Natives identified by tribal leadership should be enumerators and trainers for conducting the census in their communities.

Finally, Census 2020 and the Bureau's leadership must be free from the taint of partisanship. The census has been managed by neutral, impartial, non-partisan professionals, including Interim Director Jarmin and Interim Deputy Director Lamas, who are intimately familiar with the Bureau's operations and are well respected by Bureau staff. Through such exacting leadership, census products are accepted and form the very cornerstone of the quality data that contributes to ensuring that we have government that is representative of all the people.

NARF and its partners in the Native American Voting Rights Coalition look forward to working with this Committee to overcome the barriers in making Indian Country count in the 2020 Census. We all need to work together to get the count right.

Thank you very much for your attention, and I will welcome the opportunity to answer any questions you may have.

[The prepared statement of Mr. Tucker follows:]

PREPARED STATEMENT OF JAMES T. TUCKER, PRO BONO VOTING RIGHTS COUNSEL, NATIVE AMERICAN RIGHTS FUND [1]

Chairman Hoeven, Vice Chairman Udall, and Members of the Committee, thank you for your invitation to testify on making Indian Country count in the 2020 Census. The Native American Rights Fund (NARF) applauds the Committee for examining this important topic.

NARF is the oldest and largest nonprofit law firm dedicated to asserting and defending the rights of Indian tribes, organizations and individuals nationwide. NARF co-founded and leads the Native American Voting Rights Coalition (NAVRC), a coalition of national and regional grassroots organizations, academics, and attorneys advocating for the equal access of Native Americans to the political process. [2]

Why an Accurate Census Matters to Indian Country

The 2020 Census is one of the foremost civil rights issues in Indian Country. It serves as the keystone for our representative government in two ways. First, it determines federal apportionment under Article I, Section 2 of the U.S. Constitution, as well as state and local apportionment in non-tribal elections to meet constitutional equal population (one person, one vote) requirements. Second, decennial census data is used in redistricting to draw the lines that link representatives to their constituents for the next ten years. Past undercounts of the American Indian and Alaska Native (AIAN) populations have deprived hundreds of thousands of Native Americans of their voice in government. Without an equal voice in elections, Indian Country is deprived of access to the resources and policy decisions that are so desperately needed in some of the nation's most economically disadvantaged communities.

An accurate count also means dollars, with decennial census data serving as the basis for funding allocations for federally funded programs. Each year, nearly $600 billion in federal funds is distributed based upon population counts obtained through surveys by federal agencies. The AIAN population cannot be cut out of their access to critical federal programs because some may believe it is not expedient or cost-effective to count Native peoples living in more sparsely populated communities.

---

[1] S.J.D. and LL.M., University of Pennsylvania; J.D., University of Florida; M.P.A., University of Oklahoma; B.A., Arizona State University, Barrett Honors College. Attorney at Wilson Elser Moskowitz Edelman & Dicker LLP; Pro Bono Voting Rights Counsel to the Native American Rights Fund; Member, Census Bureau National Advisory Committee on Racial, Ethnic, and Other Populations (NAC).

[2] For more information about the NAVRC, *see* NARF, *About the Native American Voting Rights Coalition*, *available at* https://www.narf.org/native-american-voting-rights-coalition/.

<u>Overview of the American Indian and Alaska Native Population and its Undercount</u>

The AIAN population is one of the fastest growing population groups in the United States. According to the 2010 Census, the number of people identifying themselves as AIAN alone or in combination with one or more other races increased nearly three times as fast as the total U.S. population, growing by 27 percent from 4.1 million in 2000 to 5.2 million in 2010.[3] As of 2016, the AIAN population, including those of more than one race, is estimated to be 6.7 million, comprising approximately two percent of the total population.[4] By 2060, the AIAN population is projected to be 10.2 million alone or in combination with one or more other races, comprising about 2.4 percent of the estimated total population.[5]

Nearly half of all of the states have a substantial AIAN population. According to the Census Bureau, in 2016, 21 states had a population of 100,000 or more Alaska Natives or American Indian residents, alone or in combination with another race.[6] Alaska had the largest percentage of AIAN residents, who comprised 19.9 percent of the state's population in 2016. Other states in the top five included Oklahoma (13.7 percent), New Mexico (11.9 percent), South Dakota (10.4 percent) and Montana (8.4 percent).[7] In 2016, California had the largest estimated AIAN population, with nearly 1.1 million AIAN residents.[8] American Indians and Alaska Natives reside in every region of the United States, whether rural or urban.

Despite their growth, the AIAN population continues to experience the largest census undercount of any population group. The Census Bureau estimates that American Indians and Alaska Natives living on reservations or in Native villages were undercounted by approximately 4.9 percent in 2010, more than double the undercount rate of the next closest population group.[9] The undercount occurred in 2010 despite the Census Bureau's "special emphasis ... on outreach

---

[3] U.S. Census Bureau, Population Division, 2010 Census Briefs, The American Indian and Alaska Native Population: 2010, at 3-4 (Jan. 2012).

[4] U.S. Census Bureau, Population Division, Annual Estimates of the Resident Population by Sex, Age, Race and Hispanic Origin for the United States and States: 2016 Population Estimates. Table PEPASR5H (June 2017).

[5] U.S. Census Bureau, Population Division, Table 10, Projections of the Population by Sex, Hispanic Origin, and Race for the United States: 2015 to 2060 (NP2014-T10) (Dec. 2014).

[6] U.S. Census Bureau, Population Division, Annual Estimates of the Resident Population by Sex, Age, Race Alone or in Combination, and Hispanic Origin for the United States and States: April 1, 2010 to July 1, 2016 (June 2017) ("2016 AIAN Estimates"). The 21 states were Alaska, Arizona, California, Colorado, Florida, Georgia, Illinois, Michigan, Minnesota, New Jersey, New Mexico, New York, North Carolina, Ohio, Oklahoma, Oregon, Pennsylvania, Texas, Virginia, Washington and Wisconsin. *See id.*

[7] U.S. Census Bureau, Facts for Features: American Indian and Alaska Native Heritage Month: November 2017 (Oct. 6, 2017), *available at* https://www.census.gov/newsroom/facts-for-features/2017/aian-month.html ("2017 AIAN Summary").

[8] 2016 AIAN Estimates, *supra* note 6, for California.

[9] U.S. Census Bureau, 2010 Census Coverage Measurement Results News Conference, PowerPoint Presentation 19 (May 22, 2012), *available at* https://www.census.gov/2010census/news/pdf/20120512_ccm_newsconf_slides.pdf. The Census Bureau has determined that the 2010 undercount for the on-reservation AIAN population is significantly different from the 2000 Census. *Id.*

to those living on reservations and in Alaska Native villages and communities, a population that has been historically undercounted."[10]

There are Many Reasons for the Undercount of American Indians and Alaska Natives

Members of the 567 federally recognized tribes[11] are more vulnerable than other groups to being undercounted because of the many unique challenges they face. Tribal members who live on reservations or in Alaska Native villages may be geographically isolated. Native communities overwhelmingly have smaller populations and reside in Hard-to-Count Census Tracts, which necessitates techniques including Nonresponse Follow-Up (preferably in-person), larger sample sizes, and oversampling among other things. A variety of other barriers exist to accurate enumeration, some of which are unique to the American Indian and Alaska Native population.

Historical distrust of the federal government:

As a starting point, one of the most significant barriers to enumeration by the Census Bureau is the bad relationship the AIAN population has had, and continues to have, with the federal government. Antipathy and distrust persist towards Federal, State, and local governments because of past (and in some cases, ongoing) actions that discriminate against Natives or that undermine the preservation of their culture and heritage. One recent example of a federal action contributing to this distrust is the Administration's unlawful action in revoking and replacing the Bears Ears National Monument on December 4, 2017,[12] despite the years of efforts by the Tribal Governments in and around Bears Ears to get the National Monument established.[13] Another is the Administration's revival of the Dakota Access and Keystone XL Pipelines, which were approved in spite of the dangers they pose to local water supplies and sacred burial grounds of Native peoples in the Dakotas, Iowa, and Nebraska.[14]

In the fall of 2016 and spring of 2017, NAVRC oversaw one of the most comprehensive in-person surveys ever conducted in Indian Country about barriers faced by Native voters. A

---

[10] U.S. Census Bureau, Tribal Consultation Handbook: Background Materials for Tribal Consultations on the 2020 Census 20 (Fall 2015) (noting that the AIAN Program was changed for the 2000 Census "to address an undercount from the 1990 Census, and to respect the diversity of each tribe"), *available at* https://www.census.gov/content/dam/Census/library/publications/2015/dec/2020_tribal_consultation_handbook.pdf.

[11] U.S. Dep't of the Interior, Bureau of Indian Affairs, Indian Entities Recognized and Eligible To Receive Services From the United States Bureau of Indian Affairs, 82 Fed. Reg. 4,915 to 4,920 (Jan. 17, 2017) (listing federally recognized tribes and Alaska Native villages).

[12] *See* The White House, Presidential Proclamation Modifying the Bears Ears National Monument (Dec. 4, 2017), *available at* https://www.whitehouse.gov/presidential-actions/presidential-proclamation-modifying-bears-ears-national-monument/.

[13] *See* NARF, Protecting Bears Ears National Monument, *available at* https://www.narf.org/cases/protecting-bears-ears-national-monument/ (providing an overview of Bears Ears and a copy of the Complaint filed by NARF on behalf of the Tribes to stop the Administration's unlawful proclamation).

[14] *See* NARF, Trump Signs Presidential Memoranda to Revive Dakota Access and Keystone XL Pipelines (Jan 25, 2017), *available at* https://www.narf.org/trump-signs-presidential-memoranda-revive-dakota-access-keystone-xl-pipelines/.

total of 2,800 Native voters in four states completed the in-person survey.[15] In all four states, Native voters expressed the greatest trust in their Tribal Governments. Although the federal government was identified by respondents as the most trusted of non-tribal governments (federal, state, local), the level of trust ranged from a high of just 28 percent in Nevada to a low of only 16.3 percent in South Dakota.[16] Those negative experiences often deter responses to government inquiries.

Moreover, even when federal officials engage in outreach to Tribal Governments, their engagement often lacks the cultural sensitivity necessary to be effective. For example, at NAVRC's Portland field hearing on the state of voting rights in Indian Country, a member of the Yakama Tribe explained the impact of having non-Native trainers.[17] He attended a Census meeting in which a non-Native trainer purported to explain to the Native enumerators what steps they needed to take to be culturally appropriate for their interactions with Native respondents. The Yakama tribal member walked out of the meeting while it was still in progress. When another attendee asked why, he responded that it was inappropriate for a non-Native person to tell him about his own Native culture. Another pervasive example of the lack of sensitivity occurs when federal officials show up on tribal lands, unannounced and without an invitation from the Tribal Government.

Geographical isolation and inclement weather conditions:

Geography is a difficult barrier for the Census to overcome in its enumeration efforts in Indian Country.

Approximately one-third of the total AIAN population lives in Hard-to-Count Census Tracts – roughly 1.7 million out of 5.3 million people from the 2011-2015 American Community Survey (ACS) estimates.[18] Hard-to-Count Census Tracts include those Census Tracts "in the bottom 20 percent of 2010 Census Mail Return Rates (i.e. Mail Return Rates of 73 percent or less) or tracts for which a mail return rate is not applicable because they are enumerated in 2010 using the special Update/Enumerate method."[19] The states with the greatest percentage of the

---

[15] *See* The Native American Voting Rights Coalition, Survey Research Report: Voting Barriers Encountered by Native Americans in Arizona, New Mexico, Nevada and South Dakota 8, 38, 67 (Jan. 2018) ("NAVRC Report"), *available at* https://www.narf.org/wordpress/wp-content/uploads/2018/01/2017NAVRCsurvey-results.pdf. The Executive Summary of the NAVRC Report is available at https://www.narf.org/wordpress/wp-content/uploads/2018/01/2017NAVRCsurvey-summary.pdf. The survey respondents included 644 Native voters in Arizona, 1,052 in Nevada, 602 in New Mexico, and 502 in South Dakota. NAVRC Report, *supra*, at 8, 38, 67.

[16] *See* NAVRC Report, *supra* note 15, at 15, 45, 77, 111. Respondents were asked, "Which government do you trust most to protect your rights?" *Id.* at 15, 45, 76-77. Among respondents in the other two states, 22.1 percent identified the federal government in Arizona and 27.4 percent identified the federal government in New Mexico. *See id.* at 77, 111.

[17] For more information about the NAVRC's field hearings, *see* NARF, Voting Rights Hearings, *available at* https://www.narf.org/voting-rights-hearings/.

[18] *See* The Leadership Conference Education Fund. Table 1a: States Ranked by Number of American Indian/Alaska Natives (race alone or combination) living in Hard-to-Count (HTC) Census Tracts, *available at* http://civilrightsdocs.info/pdf/census/2020/Table1a-States-Number-AIAN-HTC.pdf.

[19] *Id.*

AIAN population in Hard-to-Count Census Tracts reside in the western states: New Mexico (78.6 percent), Arizona (68.1 percent), and Alaska (65.6 percent).[20] Geographical isolation plays one of the most significant reasons for why those states have such a large percentage of their AIAN population in Hard-to-Count areas.

Alaska presents a particularly compelling example of how geographical barriers impact accurate enumeration. The logical starting point for that example is to illustrate the sheer size of the largest state:

Figure 1. Comparison of the Size of Alaska to the Continental United States.

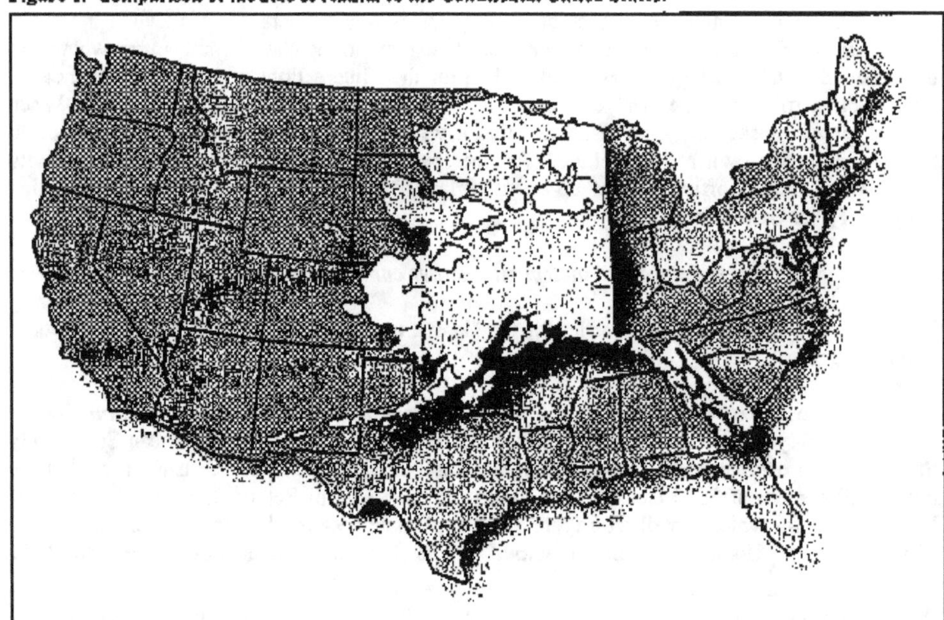

Despite its size, the rural areas of Alaska generally are very sparsely populated. As an example, NARF brought a voting rights action on behalf of the largest group of Yup'ik-speaking Alaska Natives: those residing in villages in the Bethel Census Area. The Bethel Census Area covers an area of over 40.5 million square miles[21] or roughly the size of the state of Tennessee.[22]

---

[23] *See* The Leadership Conference Education Fund, Table 1b: States Ranked by Percent of American Indian/Alaska Natives (race alone or combination) living in Hard-to-Count (HTC) Census Tracts, *available at* http://civilrightsdocs.info/pdf/census/2020/Table1b-States-Percent-AIAN-HTC.pdf.

[21] U.S. Census Bureau, QuickFacts: Bethel Census Area, Alaska ("BCA QuickFacts"), *available at* https://www.census.gov/quickfacts/fact/table/bethelcensusareaalaska/PST045216.

[22] *See* U.S. Census Bureau, QuickFacts: Tennessee ("Tennessee QuickFacts"), *available at* https://www.census.gov/quickfacts/TN.

However, in 2016, the Bethel Census Area had a total estimated population of just 17,968, a population density of just 0.4 persons per square mile.[23]

Nearly all of rural Alaska, which is dominated by Alaska Native communities, is not on the state road system. Access to those communities is typically by air or by boat. In the winter months, when the conditions permit, villages also may be connected by "ice roads," which are traversed by snowmobile or ATVs that travel on frozen rivers. For communities that are not regional "hubs" like Bethel and Dillingham, air services are provided by "bush pilots" who use runways that are little more than gravel roads. Flights are limited to Visual Flight Rules (VFR) conditions when the rough-hewn runways are not iced over.

Because of the limited accessibility to over 200 geographically isolated rural and Alaska Native communities, travel is much more constrained by the dominant weather conditions than any other location in the continental United States. It is not unusual for villages to be inaccessible by air for several weeks due to inclement weather, icing conditions, and above all fog. During the Alaska voting rights litigation in which I have served as co-counsel, I have experienced these conditions first-hand. Flights have been cancelled or delayed even under the best weather conditions, when the fog may linger late into the day.

Geography and weather have a tremendous impact on the mail service, which historically has played a key role in Census enumeration efforts. The extraordinary efforts that postal workers make to deliver mail to isolated Alaska Native villages are truly commendable. But rural Alaska may be one of the few places in the world in which the immortal words of Herodotus do not always ring true: "Neither snow, nor rain, nor heat, nor gloom of night, stays these couriers from the swift completion of their appointed rounds." Unpredictable weather conditions in the outer reaches of Alaska always have the final say in the delivery and pick-up of mail, including the critical communications being sent by the Census Bureau regarding its enumeration and data-gathering programs.

While the geographical challenges to reaching the AIAN population in Alaska can be extreme, they are not unique to Alaska. The Havasupai Indian Reservation in Arizona, which is located at the bottom of the Grand Canyon, is among the nation's most isolated reservations. The Red Lake Indian Reservation in northwestern Minnesota, which has the state's second largest AIAN population, is separated from much of the rest of the state. Many reservations are located far from urban areas and are connected (if at all) by roads that are susceptible to changing weather conditions.[24] Unpaved and poor driving conditions add to the isolation that is part of the daily lives of much of the AIAN population residing on rural reservations.

---

[23] *See* BCA QuickFacts, *supra* note 21. That compares to a population density of 153.9 persons per square mile in Tennessee. *See* Tennessee QuickFacts, *supra* note 22.

[24] *See generally* Rosanda Suetopka, *Wet Weather Wreaks Havoc on Rez Bus Routes*, NAVAJO-HOPI OBSERVER (Dec. 16, 2014) ("Road conditions on both Navajo and Hopi reservations become extremely tricky and dangerous in the wintertime causing expensive repair work on personal and school vehicles. The vehicles travel over deeply mud-rutted and pot-holed roads, which have been damaged by snow and rain, ruining and damaging wheel alignment and tires."), *available at* https://www.nhonews.com/news/2014/dec/16/wet-weather-wreaks-havoc-on-rez-bus-routes/.

Non-traditional mailing addresses and homelessness:

The 2015 National Content Test (NCT) Report illustrates the many challenges the Census Bureau and other federal agencies face in the accurate enumeration of the AIAN population.[25] *Among all of the population groups included in the 2015 NCT, the AIAN population experienced the lowest 2010 Census mail response rate, at 57.8 percent.*[26] The lack of mailing addresses for many Native peoples on tribal lands had an impact on how the 2015 NCT was conducted in Indian Country. As the Census Bureau explained, its report "includes only self-responders in areas with relatively high address mailability. Recall that the 2015 NCT did not include a Nonresponse Followup operation or any enumeration of areas with high concentrations of nonmailable addresses."[27] Although this was a significant limitation of the 2015 NCT, it offers an accurate representation of the challenges in counting many AIAN persons and households.

Two contributing factors to low mail response rates in Indian Country are lack of traditional mailing addresses and homelessness.

Non-traditional mailing addresses are prevalent among American Indians and Alaska Natives residing on tribal lands. Non-traditional mailing addresses encompass "noncity-style addresses, which the Census Bureau defines as those that do not contain a house number and/or a street name."[28] Examples of noncity-style mailing addresses include:

- General delivery
- Rural route and box number
- Highway contract route and box number
- Post office box only delivery

Noncity-style addresses used by the Census Bureau also include location descriptions such as "BRICK HOUSE with ATTACHED GARAGE ON RIGHT," structure points (geographic coordinates), and census geographic codes including state code, county code, census tract number, and census block number.[29]

It is commonplace for homes on tribal lands to use noncity-style mailing addresses. Many homes can only be identified by a geographic location (e.g., "hogan located three miles

---

[25] *See* U.S. Census Bureau, 2015 National Content Test Race and Ethnicity Analysis Report (Feb. 28, 2017) ("NCT Report").

[26] *Id.* at 32, table 2.

[27] *Id.* at 58.

[28] U.S. Census Bureau, 2020 Census Local Update of Census Addresses Program Improvement Project Recommendations 2 (Apr. 13, 2015) ("2020 LUCA Recommendations"), *available at* https://www2.census.gov/geo/pdfs/partnerships/2020_luca_recommendation.pdf.

[29] *Id.*

down dirt road from Hardrock Chapter House"). Others may be located by reference to a BIA, state, or county road mile marker (e.g., "the house located on the right side of BIA-41 between highway marker 17 and highway marker 18") or intersection (e.g., the house at the intersection of BIA-41 and BIA-15"). Additionally, mailboxes may be on the side of the road far from where the home(s) associated with them are located, with the mailbox identified only by a General Delivery number, Rural Route, or box number. Many AIAN residents of tribal lands only receive their mail by post office box. Often, several families or generations of a single family might share a post office or general delivery box to get their mail.

At the NAVRC field hearings on voting rights, several AIAN witnesses have testified about how their use of a non-traditional mailing address has either made it difficult to register to vote or has disenfranchised them altogether. This testimony has been consistent throughout Indian Country, regardless of the location of the tribal lands:

- At the Bismarck, North Dakota field hearing, an elected county official testified that many voters residing on the Crow Creek Indian Reservation in Buffalo County, South Dakota have had difficulty registering to vote because of non-traditional addresses. That problem persisted even after efforts were undertaken to identify physical addresses to use in the County's 911-emergency notification system.

- At the Portland, Oregon field hearing, voters from the Colville and Yakama Reservations in eastern Washington State testified that many tribal members were unable to register to vote to receive their ballot by mail for state elections because they only had post office boxes available that could not be readily correlated with a physical address where they actually lived.

- At the San Diego field hearing, a member of the Torrez Martinez Desert Cahuilla Indian, located just west of the Salton Sea in California, did not have a traditional mailing address and was only able to vote because of the timely intervention of a family friend who was running for office and was able to get a waiver of the registration requirement for a physical address.

NARF is currently litigating this very issue in North Dakota,[30] where the state legislature enacted a restrictive voter identification law that requires that acceptable identification cards must contain a registrant's residential address — which most tribal members living on tribal lands do not have because of their use of non-traditional mailing addresses.[31] The same barriers that AIAN persons with non-traditional mailing addresses experience in attempting to register to vote make it difficult for them to be identified by Census enumerators.

---

[30] *See Brakebill v. Jaeger*, Civil Action No. 1:16-cv-00008-DLH-CSM (Am. Compl. filed Dec. 13, 2017).

[31] *See* NARF, Brakebill, et al. v. Jaeger (ND Voter ID Law), *available at* https://www.narf.org/cases/nd-voter-id/.

The disproportionately high rate of homelessness in Indian Country is another major factor contributing to low mailing response rates among the AIAN population. According to the 2016 ACS, only 52.9 percent of single-race American Indian and Alaska Native householders owned their own home, compared to 63.1 percent of the total population.[32] According to data from the U.S. Department of Housing and Urban Development, although "only 1.2 percent of the national population self-identifies as AI/AN … 4.0 percent of all sheltered homeless persons, 4.0 percent of all sheltered homeless individuals, and 4.8 percent of all sheltered homeless families self-identify as Native American or Alaska Native."[33] The AIAN population likewise experiences higher rates of homelessness among veterans than other population groups. Specifically, "2.5 percent of sheltered, homeless Veterans were American Indian or Alaska Native, although only 0.7 percent of all Veterans are American Indian or Alaska Native."[34]

Homelessness takes several forms in Indian Country. Witnesses at the NAVRC field hearings in Portland and San Diego testified that it is common for younger AIAN persons to frequently change residence. Those practices can vary from "crashing on a couch" of a friend or classmate, to temporarily sleeping at a relative's house when they are on the reservation. According to the 2016 ACS, approximately 15.5 percent of the AIAN population was residing in a different house than the one they reported a year earlier.[35] Frequently changing residences, with no single permanent residence, can make many American Indians and Alaska Natives harder to locate.[36]

The top five locations with the largest number of AIAN people living in Hard-to-Count Census Tracts are all in urban areas: New York City (44,760 people); Phoenix (21,398 people); Oklahoma City (19,826 people); Los Angeles (19,056 people); and Anchorage (14,151 people).[37] Similarly, the top five locations with the largest percentage of AIAN people living in Hard-to-Count Census Tracts are in large cities: Newark (97.5 percent); Jersey City (94.7 percent); New Orleans (86.9 percent); Buffalo (82.2 percent); and Paradise CDP, part of unincorporated Las

---

[32] 2017 AIAN Summary, *supra* note 7.

[33] Substance Abuse and Mental Health Services Administration (SAMHSA), Expert Panel on Homelessness among American Indians, Alaska Natives, and Native Hawaiians 5 (2012), *available at* https://www.usich.gov/resources/uploads/asset_library/Expert_Panel_on_Homelessness_among_American_Indians%2C_Alaska_Natives%2C_and_Native_Hawaiians.pdf.

[34] *Id.* at 8 (citing HUD & VA, Veteran Homelessness: A Supplemental Report to the 2010 Annual Homeless Assessment Report to Congress).

[35] *See* U.S. Census Bureau, 2016 American Community Survey 1-Year Estimates, Selected Population Profile in the United States: American Indian and Alaska Native alone (300, A01-Z99) ("2016 AIAN Profile"), *available at* https://factfinder.census.gov/faces/tableservices/jsf/pages/productview.xhtml?src=bkmk.

[36] U.S. Department of Housing and Urban Development, "Housing Needs of American Indians and Alaska Natives in Tribal Areas: A Report From the Assessment of American Indian, Alaska Native, and Native Hawaiian Housing Needs (Jan. 2017), *available at* https://www.huduser.gov/portal/sites/default/files/pdf/HNAIHousingNeeds.pdf.

[37] *See* The Leadership Conference Education Fund, Table 2a: Largest Places Ranked by Number of American Indian/Alaska Natives (race alone or combination) living in Hard-to-Count (HTC) Census Tracts, *available at* http://civilrightsdocs.info/pdf/census/2020/Table2a-100-Largest-Places-Number-AIAN-HTC.pdf.

Vegas (67.5 percent).[38] Urban Indians often reside in Hard-to-Count Census Tracts because of depressed socio-economic characteristics, which they share in common with other population groups residing in those Tracts.[39]

Socio-economic barriers:

Socio-economic barriers likewise make the AIAN population harder for enumerators to reach. Native peoples have the highest poverty rate of any population group, 26.6 percent, which is nearly double the poverty rate of the nation as a whole.[40] The poverty rate was even higher on federally recognized Indian reservations and Alaska Native villages, at 38.3 percent.[41] The median household income of single-race American Indian and Alaska Native households in 2016 was $39,719, far below the national median household income of $57,617.[42]

The AIAN population also has lower rates of educational attainment, which impacts their participation in the Census. Among the AIAN population 25 years of age and older, 20.1 percent had less than a high school education.[43] The unemployment rate of those aged 16 and older in the workforce was 12 percent.[44] Approximately 19.2 percent lacked health insurance,[45] and 13.4 percent of all occupied households lacked access to a vehicle.[46]

Age:

Younger populations typically are harder to count than older populations in the Census. To illustrate that fact, in the 2010 Census, the net undercount for young children was 4.6 percent,[47] very close to the undercount rate of approximately 4.9 percent for American Indians

---

[38] *See* The Leadership Conference Education Fund, Table 2b: Largest Places Ranked by Percent of American Indian/Alaska Natives (race alone or combination) living in Hard-to-Count (HTC) Census Tracts, *available at* http://civilrightsdocs.info/pdf/census/2020/Table2b-100-Largest-Places-Percent-AIAN-HTC.pdf.

[39] For an excellent article describing the challenges faces by urban Indians, *see* Joe Whittle, *Most Native Americans Live in Cities, Not Reservations. Here are Their Stories.* THE GUARDIAN (U.S. EDITION) (Sept. 4, 2017), *available at* https://www.theguardian.com/us-news/2017/sep/04/native-americans-stories-california.

[40] U.S. Census Bureau, Profile America Facts for Features: CB16-FF.22, American Indian and Alaska Native statistics, *available at* https://www.census.gov/newsroom/facts-for-features/2016/cb16-ff22.html (Nov. 2, 2016) ("2016 AIAN FFF").

[41] U.S. Census Bureau, Table B17001C: Selected Population Profile in the United States: 2015 American Community Survey 1-Year Estimates (last visited on Feb. 7, 2018), *available at* https://factfinder.census.gov/bkmk/table/1.0/en/ACS/15_1YR/B17001C/0100000US|01000089US.

[42] 2017 AIAN Summary, *supra* note 7.

[43] *See* 2016 AIAN Profile, *supra* note 35.

[44] *Id.*

[45] *Id.*

[46] *Id.*

[47] *See* U.S. Census Bureau, Decennial Statistics Studies Division, Investigating the 2010 Undercount of Young Children – A New Look at 2010 Census Omissions by Age 1 (July 26, 2016), *available at* https://www2.census.gov/programs-surveys/decennial/2020/program-management/memo-series/2020-report-2010-undercount-children-ommissions.pdf.

and Alaska Natives residing on tribal lands.[48] Among all American Indians and Alaska Natives, the median age is over five years younger than the median age for the total population.[49] For American Indians and Alaska Natives living on reservations or in Alaska Native villages, the difference in median age with the total population is nearly nine years.[50]

According to the 2016 ACS, 27.4 percent of all American Indians and Alaska Natives are under 18 years of age.[51] Approximately one-third of the AIAN population under 18 years of age, 33.8 percent, is below the poverty line.[52] The depressed socio-economic status of some of these children makes it harder to obtain an accurate count of them in the Census.

Language barriers and illiteracy among LEP Tribal Elders:

Dozens of different dialects are widely spoken among the major AIAN languages. Over a quarter of all single-race American Indian and Alaska Natives speak a language other than English at home.[53] Two-thirds of all speakers of American Indian or Alaska Native languages reside on a reservation or in a Native village,[54] including many who are linguistically isolated, have limited English skills, or a high rate of illiteracy.[55]

Nationally, 357,409 AIAN persons reside in a jurisdiction covered by Section 203 of the Voting Rights Act, where assistance must be provided in the covered Native language.[56] Alaska Native language assistance is required in 15 political subdivisions of Alaska, which "is an increase of 8 political subdivisions from 2011."[57] Assistance in American Indian languages is required in 35 political subdivisions in nine states, "up from the 33 political subdivisions of five states covered in the 2011 determinations."[58]

---

[48] *See supra* note 9.

[49] *Compare* U.S. Census Bureau, Table B01002C: Median Age by Sex (American Indian and Alaska Native) (American Indian and Alaska Native median age of 32.5 years), *available at* https://factfinder.census.gov/bkmk/table/1.0/en/ACS/15_1YR/B01002C, *with* U.S. Census Bureau, Table S0101: Age and Sex (median age of 37.8 years for the total population), *available at* https://factfinder.census.gov/bkmk/table/1.0/en/ACS/15_1YR/S0101.

[50] *See* U.S. Census Bureau, American FactFinder, Table B01002C, Median Age by Sex (American Indian and Alaska Native), American Indian Reservation and Trust Land, 2016 ACS 1-Year Estimates (28.8 years), *available at* https://factfinder.census.gov/bkmk/table/1.0/en/ACS/15_1YR/B01002C/0100000US|0100089US.

[51] *See* 2016 AIAN Profile, *supra* note 35.

[52] *Id.*

[53] 2016 AIAN FFF, *supra* note 40 (27 percent).

[54] *See* U.S. Census Bureau, Native American Languages Spoken at Home in the United States and Puerto Rico: 2006-2010 at 2 (Dec. 2011).

[55] *See* U.S. Census Bureau, Public Use Data File for the 2016 Determinations under Section 203 of the Voting Rights Act, *available at* https://www.census.gov/rdo/data/voting_rights_determination_file.html (Dec. 5, 2016).

[56] U.S. Census Bureau, Press Release: Census Bureau Releases 2016 Determinations for Section 203 of the Voting Rights Act (Dec. 5, 2016), *available at* https://www.census.gov/newsroom/press-releases/2016/cb16-205.html.

[57] AAJC, NALEO & NARF, Voting Rights Act Coverage Update 3 (Dec. 2016) ("Section 203 Update"), *available at* https://advancingjustice-aajc.org/sites/default/files/2016-12/Section%20203%20Coverage%20Update.pdf.

[58] *Id.*

Alaska, Arizona, and New Mexico have the largest number of Limited-English Proficient (LEP) persons voting-age citizens (that is, U.S. citizens who are 18 years of age and older). Between them, they account for approximately 87 percent of all American Indians and Alaska Natives who reside in an area required to provide language assistance in an Alaska Native or American Indian language:

Figure 2. Comparison Between the Top Three States with Limited-English Proficient AIAN Populations.

Alaska	Arizona	New Mexico
54,275 Alaska Natives live in one of the 15 areas covered by Section 203 for an Alaska Native language.	123,470 American Indians live in one of the six counties covered by Section 203 for an American Indian language.	132,955 American Indians live in one of the 10 counties covered by Section 203 for an American Indian language.
At least 10 percent of all Alaska Natives in covered areas are of voting age and LEP in an Alaska Native language.	At least 14.5 percent of all American Indians in covered areas are of voting age and LEP in an American Indian language.	At least 8 percent of all American Indians in covered areas are of voting age and LEP in an American Indian language.
LEP Alaska Natives are located in approximately 200 villages and communities in the 15 covered areas.	Approximately 96.7 percent of all American Indians who are LEP and reside in a county covered for Native language assistance reside in just three counties: Apache, Coconino, and Navajo.	91.1 percent of all American Indians and 89.3 percent of all voting-age American Indians who are LEP and live in a covered county live in just four counties: Bernalillo, McKinley, Sandoval, and San Juan.

Language poses a barrier to successful enumeration for several reasons. First, LEP American Indians and Alaska Natives, like other LEP populations, are generally among the hardest to reach within the Hard-to-Count population. Outreach and publicity communications written or transmitted in English usually are not understood unless they are translated into the applicable Native language. In-person communication through trained bilingual enumerators yields the best results, but can be confounded by the lack of enumerators fluent in the language, geography, and adequate funding to reach the LEP population.

Moreover, the difficulty in preparing complete, accurate, and uniform translations of survey tools (including instructions and questions) is compounded by the absence of words in Native languages for many English terms. Frequently, that requires that concepts be translated to communicate the meaning of what is being asked, rather than word-for-word translations. Identification of those concepts usually requires closely coordinating with trained linguists from Native communities to provide effective translations. It simply is not possible for Federal agencies to use a "one-size-fits-all" approach in creating and using survey instruments in Indian Country, including the Census enumeration.

Illiteracy also is very prevalent among LEP American Indians and Alaska Natives, especially among Tribal Elders. In areas covered by Section 203 of the Voting Rights Act, illiteracy among LEP voting-age citizens is many times higher than the national illiteracy rate of 1.31 percent in 2016.[59]

In Alaska, in covered areas for which Census data is available, the illiteracy rate among LEP Alaska Natives of voting age is 40 percent for Aleut-speakers, 28.4 percent for Athabascan-speakers, 15 percent for Yup'ik-speakers, and 8.2 percent for Inupiat-speakers.[60] In Arizona, in covered areas for which Census data is available, the illiteracy rate among LEP American Indians of voting age is 25 percent for Navajo-speakers and 6.8 percent for Apache-speakers.[61] In Mississippi, in covered areas for which Census data is available, the illiteracy rate among LEP American Indians of voting age is 34 percent for Choctaw-speakers.[62] Finally, in New Mexico, in covered areas for which Census data is available, the illiteracy rate among LEP American Indians of voting age is 19.1 percent for Navajo-speakers and 6.7 percent for Apache-speakers; data was not available for speakers of the Pueblo languages.[63]

In areas with LEP Tribal Elders who are hampered by illiteracy, enumeration generally must be done in-person by a bilingual enumerator fully fluent in the Native language and applicable dialect.

Lack of broadband access and Internet use:

In response to the growing use of technology among the general population, Census 2020 enumeration "will offer the opportunity and encourage people to respond via the Internet..."[64] However, the digital divide is most profoundly felt among the AIAN population. People residing

---

[59] *See* U.S. Census Bureau, Flowchart of How the Law Prescribes the Determination of Covered Areas under the Language Minority Provisions of Section 203 of the Voting Rights Act 2 (Dec. 5, 2016), *available at* https://www.census.gov/rdo/pdf/2_PrescribedFlowFor203Determinations.pdf. "Illiteracy" is defined as including those persons who "have less than a 5th grade education." *Id.*

[60] *See* U.S. Census Bureau, Voting Rights Determination File: Section 203 Determinations (Dec. 5, 2016), Public Use Data File and Technical Documentation (Excel spreadsheet of "Determined Areas Only") ("Section 203 Determination File"), *available at* https://www.census.gov/rdo/data/voting_rights_determination_file.html. In Alaska, the illiteracy rate among LEP voting-age citizens in covered areas compares to the national illiteracy rate of 1.31 percent as follows: 30.5 times higher for Aleut-speakers; 21.7 times higher for Athabascan-speakers; 11.4 times higher for Yup'ik-speakers; and 6.3 times higher for Inupiat-speakers. *Compare id. with supra* note 59 and accompanying text.

[61] *See* Section 203 Determination File, *supra* note 60. In Arizona, the illiteracy rate among LEP voting-age citizens in covered areas compares to the national illiteracy rate of 1.31 percent as follows: 19.1 times higher for Navajo-speakers; and 5.2 times higher for Apache-speakers. *Compare id. with supra* note 59 and accompanying text.

[62] *See* Section 203 Determination File, *supra* note 60. In Mississippi, the illiteracy rate among LEP voting-age citizens in covered areas compares to the national illiteracy rate of 1.31 percent as follows: 25.9 times higher for Choctaw-speakers. *Compare id. with supra* note 59 and accompanying text.

[63] *See* Section 203 Determination File, *supra* note 60. In New Mexico, the illiteracy rate among LEP voting-age citizens in covered areas compares to the national illiteracy rate of 1.31 percent as follows: 14.6 times higher for Navajo-speakers; and 6.7 times higher for Apache-speakers. *Compare id. with supra* note 59 and accompanying text.

[64] U.S. Census Bureau, 2020 Census Operational Plan: A New Design for the 21st Century 8 (version 3.0) (Sept. 2017), *available at* https://www2.census.gov/programs-surveys/decennial/2020/program-management/planning-docs/2020-oper-plan3.pdf.

in tribal areas have virtually no access to computers or the Internet, with the Federal Trade Commission estimating broadband penetration in tribal communities at less than ten percent.[65] Not surprisingly, the hardest to count areas for the rural AIAN population are all on reservations or in Alaska Native villages lacking reliable and affordable broadband access. To illustrate that fact, a mapping tool shows how Hard-to-Count Census Tracts correlate with reservations.[66]

During Tribal Consultations between the Census Bureau and tribal members, the Bureau received feedback that "[s]ome tribes reported that internet response is currently not a viable option for members and requested an in-person enumerator – specifically a local, tribal person."[67] In particular, connectivity was reported to be an issue "in rural areas including Alaska, Navajo Nation, Pueblos [in New Mexico]."[68] Even where some broadband access may be available, depressed socio-economic conditions often prevent American Indians and Alaska Natives from having access to or using online resources including the Internet. For example, the cost or inconvenience of driving to a location where Internet access can be obtained, or the cost of getting Internet service in those areas in Indian Country where it may be offered, prevents many American Indians and Alaska Natives from going online.[69]

The digital divide is also a generational phenomenon in Indian Country. In NAVRC's field hearing in Bismarck, we heard testimony from Montana tribal members who described the widespread use of the Internet and smart phones by younger tribal members. Similarly, the Census Bureau was informed in its Tribal Consultations that while tribes are increasingly using social media to connect with tribal members, those resources are often not generally accessible by Tribal Elders. For online enumeration, Census was informed that where broadband is available, the "younger generation will go online and respond."[70] Therefore, any enumeration of tribal lands and those for whom technology is less accessible – particularly Elders – must have alternatives that account for lack of broadband access and use.

Statistical sampling challenges caused by smaller populations:

For those Census programs that rely upon statistical sampling methods, small populations in very sparsely populated areas and communities are another significant challenge the Census Bureau faces in attempting to obtain an accurate count in Indian Country. This issue is most prevalent in the ACS and its related products.

---

[65] Parkhurst et al., The Digital Reality: E-Government and Access to Technology and Internet for American Indian and Alaska Native Populations 3, *available at* https://pdfs.semanticscholar.org/4hb4/f5efed1ef4ec342h5d45dd824bb10d9bb0f2.pdf.

[66] *See* Mapping Hard to Count (HTC) Communities for a Fair and Accurate 2020 Census, *available at* http://www.censushardtocountmaps2020.us/.

[67] *See* U.S. Census Bureau, Office of Congressional and Intergovernmental Affairs, PowerPoint Presentation, Briefing on American Indian Alaska Natives 2020 Tribal Consultation Meetings 10 (May 26, 2016) ("Tribal Consultations"), *available at* https://www2.census.gov/cac/nac/meetings/2016-05/2016-alexander.pdf.

[68] *Id.*

[69] *See* Gerry Smith, *On Tribal Lands, Digital Divide Brings New Form of Isolation*, HUFFPOST, Apr. 23, 2012, *available at* https://www.huffingtonpost.com/2012/04/20/digital-divide-tribal-lands_n_1403046.html

[70] Tribal Consultations, *supra* note 67, at 10.

The challenge of surveying small populations became particularly apparent following the dramatic loss of coverage for American Indian languages in the 2011 Section 203 determinations issued by the Census Bureau. In those determinations, the Census Bureau acknowledged that "the sampling error or uncertainty of the estimates of the characteristics needed for Section 203 is a weakness particularly for jurisdictions with small (ACS) samples within the period 2005-2009," the period used for the 2011 Determinations.[71] Under previous determinations, the Census Bureau used the decennial long form questionnaire sent to one in six U.S. households; in contrast, the ACS questionnaire used in the 2011 Determinations was sent to an average of one in eight U.S. households in the 5-year sample period.[72] The use of a smaller sample of population has resulted in "larger margins of error than the long-form estimates, particularly for determinations involving the small populations defined in Section 203."[73]

This challenge to obtaining an accurate count in Indian Country may be less of an issue for the 2020 Census because of the much more comprehensive enumeration it entails compared to the ACS. Nevertheless, to the extent that the 2020 Census relies on some statistical sampling methods to impute data, it may prove to be more difficult to get estimates in Indian Country because of the sparse population in many Native communities. That limitation reinforces the importance of maximizing the enumeration of all American Indians and Alaska Natives and minimizing the use of sampling in less populated areas.

<u>Recommendations on How to Improve the Count in Indian Country</u>

At first blush, the number and complexity of factors contributing to the undercount of American Indians and Alaska Natives are overwhelming. No single solution can remove all of the barriers to obtaining an accurate count in Indian Country. Rather, a multi-faceted approach must be used for the 2020 Census. To the extent permitted under the law, the enumeration of American Indians and Alaska Natives must be pliable enough to adapt to the circumstances on the ground and the unique needs of each individual Tribe or Native community.

Before offering recommendations on how to improve Census 2020 operations in Indian Country, some comments about the Census Bureau and its staff are in order. My experience with Census Bureau personnel has been as a member of the National Advisory Committee, as a client for special tabulations I have used in voting rights litigation, and as a regular consumer of Census products. Without exception, Census staff with whom I have worked are each impartial, dedicated professionals committed to making sure that every person is counted. Their work is extraordinary. Their operations are run efficiently and effectively, even in the face of dire funding shortfalls that undercut their efforts. Census leadership and the professionals at the

---

[71] U.S. Census Bureau, Statistical Modeling Methodology for the Voting Rights Act Section 203 Language Assistance Determinations (Dec. 2011) ("Statistical Modeling"), *available at* http://www.census.gov/rdo/data/voting_rights_determination_file.html.

[72] *See* U.S. Census Bureau, Memorandum Regarding the 2011 Determinations 6 (Dec. 2011), *available at* http://www.census.gov/rdo/data/voting_rights_determination_file.html.

[73] Statistical Modeling, *supra* note 71, at 12.

Bureau should be commended for their stewardship in fulfilling their constitutional and statutory mandates.

Census 2020 operations must be adequately funded:

The single greatest threat to an accurate count in Indian Country and elsewhere is the inadequate funding of programs, testing, and support activities for the ramp-up to the 2020 Census. The final appropriation for FY 2017 funding for the Census Bureau was $1.47 billion, a shortfall of at least $164 million for the minimal level of funding necessary to keep Census programs running and to adequately prepare for the 2020 Census. The lack of funding has had a deleterious effect on several programs critical to the operation of the decennial census, including:

- The cancellation of planned field tests on the Standing Rock Reservation in North and South Dakota and on the Colville Reservation and Off-Reservation Trust land in Washington State, as well as a third test in Puerto Rico.

- The cancellation of two out of the three dress rehearsal sites in 2018 (the 2018 End-to-End Census Test), including those in Pierce County, Washington, and the Bluefield-Beckley-Oak Hill area of West Virginia, which offered the only opportunities to test special counting methods for rural areas such as those in much of Indian Country. The only dress rehearsal that will now be conducted is in Providence County, Rhode Island, an urban area with a negligible AIAN population.

- "Pauses" and modifications for key 2020 Census activities, including delayed openings of Regional Census Centers, Partnership Program activities, and preparations for outreach and publicity campaigns. These changes could greatly diminish the Bureau's ability to take an accurate, cost-effective census and is expected to increase the disproportionate undercount of American Indian and Alaska Natives, especially those living in rural, low-income, geographically isolated, and/or linguistically isolated households.

- Shifting funds from other important Census Bureau programs to cover shortfalls in activities essential to the 2020 Census.

Although recent continuing resolutions have included anomalies for increased Census funding, those funding levels still fall far short of where they need to be to obtain an accurate count in Indian Country.

The Administration's FY 2018 budget request for the Census Bureau initially was just $1.497 billion, a mere two percent ($27 million) increase over the already underfunded FY 2017 level. The Administration subsequently adjusted its request to be $1.654 billion, adding $187 million for 2020 Census activities. However, even the adjusted request is substantially less than what is needed for the decennial census ramp-up.

NARF joins the Leadership Conference and partnering organizations in recommending an appropriation for the Census Bureau of at least $1.848 billion for FY 2018. That figure reflects an increase of $164 million over the Administration's adjusted budget. It would address, in part, the impact that underfunding from FY 2017 has had on activities that are critical to Census 2020 operations, including:

- **An additional $24 million for Current Surveys and Programs.** The adjusted request would authorize a total discretionary appropriation of $270 million, equal to the amount identified by the Senate Appropriations Committee and the FY 2017 appropriation.

- **An additional $50 million for contingency operations.** This appropriation would be added to the contingency fund proposed by Commerce Secretary Ross to account for operational issues that may arise in preparation for the 2020 Census.

- **An additional $80 million for the communications campaign.** The Integrated Partnership and Communications (IPC) contract is behind schedule because of lack of funding in FY 2017. These funds are necessary to give the IPC the resources for identifying and communicating effective messages to Indian Country about the importance of participating in the 2020 Census.

- **An additional $10 million to increase the number of Partnership Specialists to 200.** Currently, there are just 43 Partnership Specialists who are responsible for all outreach and publicity for every national, state, regional, local and tribal organization. That number is woefully short of the staff needed to communicate and educate trusted partners in the American Indian and Alaska Native communities about the 2020 Census, particularly considering the factors that make the AIAN population Hard-to-Count.

NARF likewise supports the Leadership Conference's request for a 20 percent increase in the number of Area Census Offices. The increase is needed to ensure that sufficient personnel are available to conduct what is expected to be a very high need for Nonresponse Follow-Up among AIAN persons, especially those residing in Hard-to-Count Census Tracts.

Funding for field tests of the 2020 Census on tribal lands must be restored:

The cancelled Census Tests on Tribal Lands would have refined methods for counting people in tribal areas lacking street addresses, test methods of making in-person counts in AIAN households, and determine where and how to use oversampling to counteract the undercount facing Native people living on reservations and in Native villages.[74] The field tests on the Colville and Standing Rock Reservations should be restored expeditiously to refine the data collection methods in Indian Country for the 2020 Census.

The NCT Report illustrates the many challenges the Census Bureau and other federal agencies face in the enumeration of the AIAN population. *Among all of the population groups included in the 2015 NCT, the AIAN population experienced the lowest 2010 Census mail response rate, at 57.8 percent.*[75] The lack of mailing addresses for many Native peoples on tribal lands had an impact on how the 2015 NCT was conducted in Indian Country. As the Census Bureau explained, its report "includes only self-responders in areas with relatively high address mailability. Recall that the 2015 NCT did not include a Nonresponse Followup operation or any enumeration of areas with high concentrations of nonmailable addresses."[76] Similar problems will undoubtedly reoccur, which will only be exacerbated if no field tests are conducted in Indian Country in preparation for the 2020 Census.

The Federal Race and Ethnicity Standards and Census 2020 questionnaire must be updated to reflect AIAN concerns:

Another issue of particular concern to organizations and individuals advocating on behalf of the American Indian and Alaska Native community is the absence of any decision on revisions to the Federal Race and Ethnicity Standards. The Race and Ethnicity Standards used by every federal agency for surveys and statistical research – including enumeration by the Census Bureau through the decennial census and data-gathering through other periodic surveys such as the ACS – are very outdated. The Standards were last changed in 1997. They do not reflect changing demographics, nor do they account for inefficiencies that have become apparent in both the 2000 Census and 2010 Census that contributed to the undercount of the AIAN population.

NARF and other members of NAVRC were cautiously optimistic about the prospects for effective changes to the Standards when OMB published its notice inviting comments to be considered by the Federal Interagency Working Group.[77] We submitted written comments in response to the notice, agreeing with the recommendation made by career staff at the Census Bureau for a separate "write-in line to collect detailed AIAN responses, rather than the three conceptual checkboxes and a write-in line, on paper questionnaires."[78]

---

[74] U.S. Census Bureau, 2017 Census Test: Preparing for the 2020 Census, *available at* https://www.census.gov/content/dam/Census/programs-surveys/decennial/2020-census/2017%21Census%20Tests/2017_census_test/colville_factsheet.pdf.

[75] NCT Report, *supra* note 25, at 32, table 2.

[76] *Id.* at 58.

[77] *See* Office of Management and Budget, Proposals From the Federal Interagency Working Group for Revision of the Standards for Maintaining, Collecting, and Presenting Federal Data on Race and Ethnicity, 82 Fed. Reg. 12,242 (Mar. 1, 2017).

[78] *See* NCT Report, *supra* note 25, at 86.

Although it was widely expected that the Federal Interagency Working Group would issue revisions to the Federal Race and Ethnicity Standards at the end of 2017, that did not happen. Instead, to date, no update on the Standards or explanation for the delay has been forthcoming from the Working Group. That radio silence placed the Census Bureau in a tenuous position to meet its mandate under federal law. As the Bureau has explained, the "Census Bureau needed to make a decision on the design of the race and ethnicity questions by December 31, 2017 in order to prepare 2020 Census systems, and deliver the final 2020 Census question wording to Congress by March 31, 2018."[79]

As a result, currently the Census Bureau is planning on continuing "to use two separate questions for collecting data on race and ethnicity in the 2018 End-to-End Census Test, and as the proposed format for the 2020 Census."[80] It is true that despite the absence of changes to the 1997 Standards, the Bureau will make some modifications to the 2020 Census questionnaire. As the Bureau has explained, "The race and ethnicity questions include several design changes that were tested over the past decade in effort to improve the designs from the 2010 Census."[81] While that will not result in a change to the current 1997 definition of "American Indian or Alaska Native,"[82] it will result in one change on the questionnaire: "adding examples for the American Indian or Alaska Native racial category."[83]

The career staff at the Census Bureau should be applauded for their efforts to make the most out of a bad situation. They are to be commended for making what modifications they believe they can to the questionnaires being used for the 2018 End-to-End Test and the 2020 Census under the outdated 1997 Federal Race and Ethnicity Standards. However, due to the inaction by the Federal Interagency Working Group and the limitations imposed on the Bureau by federal law (and particularly the 1997 Standards), the proposed change does not go far enough for the AIAN population.

The NCT tested three approaches: separate questions on race and ethnicity; a combined question for race and ethnicity with write-in boxes; and a combined question with checkboxes. Among AIAN respondents completing the survey online, the response rate was highest for the combined question with detailed checkboxes, with 73 percent providing detailed responses. Notably, this response rate was significantly lower than the next closest population group surveyed through the Internet, Native Hawaiian and Pacific Islander, at 89.9 percent.[84]

---

[79] Albert E. Fontenot, Jr., Associate Director for Decennial Census Programs, Memorandum for Record Regarding Using Two Separate Questions for Race and Ethnicity in 2018 End-to-End Census Test and 2020 Census 1 (2020 Census Program Memorandum Series: 2018.02) (Jan. 26, 2018) ("Census Memo 2018.02").

[80] *Id.*

[81] *Id.*

[82] The 1997 Standards define the AIAN population to include a "person having origins in any of the original peoples of North and South America (including Central America), and who maintains tribal affiliation or community attachment." *Id.*

[83] *Id.*

[84] NCT Report, *supra* note 25, at 49 & table 10.

Largely because of the challenges in enumerating Native peoples residing in Hard-to-Count Census Tracts, it should be expected that a large proportion of the AIAN population will respond to the 2020 Census using a paper survey. However, the 2015 NCT report found that the response rate among AIAN persons surveyed using the paper format was lowest for the combined question with detailed checkboxes approach. Only 54.1 percent of AIAN respondents provided detailed responses using that approach, compared to 70.1 percent for the combined question with write-in response areas approach and 64.4 percent for the separate question approach.[85]

The Census Bureau has explained that the lower response rate using the paper format may have been because of the inclusion of "three additional AIAN checkboxes below the major category checkbox," namely "American Indian, Alaska Native, and Central or South American Indian." It is possible that the inclusion of these three existing OMB categories may have discouraged respondents from completing the write-in line, as the Census Bureau has suggested.[86] The write-in line was included because the Census Bureau acknowledged that if it "were to employ the six largest Indian groups and Alaska Native groups as checkboxes, they would represent only about 10 percent of the entire AIAN population." Doing so would effectively offer no means of identification for the "hundreds of very small detailed AIAN tribes, villages, and indigenous groups for which Census Bureau data is collected and tabulated."[87] That conclusion is reflected in the Bureau's finding that 68.1 percent of all AIAN persons surveyed in the 2015 NCT that provided their tribal affiliation or association in the write-in space were not members of the six largest AIAN groups.[88]

As a result, the Census Bureau noted: "Additional findings from this research indicate that it is optimal to use one write-in line to collect detailed AIAN responses, rather than the three conceptual checkboxes and a write-in line, on paper questionnaires. This research showed that the introduction of conceptual checkboxes (i.e., American Indian, Alaska Native, and Central/South American Indian) decreased detailed reporting for the AIAN category in paper data collections."[89] Unfortunately, it appears that approach will not be used for the 2020 Census because of the inaction by the Federal Interagency Working Group in failing to update the 1997 Standards.

Just as NARF did in its written comments, I agree with the approach proposed by the Census Bureau in the NCT, and recommend the following format to be used on the 2020 Census questionnaire: (1) provide a write-in line without the three checkboxes for the three AIAN categories under the 1997 OMB standards; (2) provide examples (as the 2015 NCT Report has suggested and as the Bureau has reiterated in its January 26, 2018 Memo) to allow AIAN respondents to understand what information is being requested on the write-in line; and

---

[85] *Id.* at 50 & table 11.

[86] *Id.* at 50.

[87] *Id.* at 52.

[88] *See id.* at 55 & table 14.

[89] *See id.* at 86.

(3) provide enough space to allow respondents to provide multiple responses if they identify with more than one tribe or village.

The Census Bureau provided an illustration of the suggested question format for respondents identifying as Alaska Native or American Indian:

Figure 3. Proposed AIAN Question Format for the 2020 Census Questionnaire.

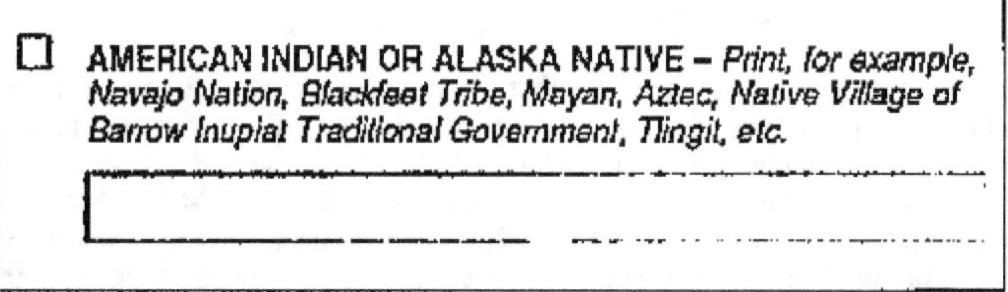

Only two modifications would need to be made to this question format. First, more lines need to be added for responses to be written in because some tribes and Native villages have long names and many respondents identify or affiliate themselves with more than one tribe or Native village. Second, input we have received at NAVRC meetings and at the field hearings indicates that two of the examples, "Mayan" and "Aztec," seem outmoded with a sparse population compared to other tribes and Native villages.

Even if the Census Bureau cannot make these changes because of the 1997 Standards, I encourage Members of Congress to authorize these changes to the question format for the 2020 Census, with any further adjustments recommended by the career professionals at the Bureau.

Perhaps even more so than other population groups, the AIAN population group is not monolithic, but instead is comprised of a broad and diverse group of distinct tribes, associations, clans, or other affiliations. Individual Native persons may self-identify differently than others within their community. Providing a write-in line is most consistent with respecting that self-identification of individuals and the Nations in which they live or with which they are affiliated. Because many Native persons belong to and identify with more than a single tribe or Native village, they must be permitted to provide all of that information in any federal survey. Furthermore, as the Census Bureau's example illustrates, even many of the single responses will require additional space to provide a response because of their length (e.g., "Native Village of Barrow Inupiat Traditional Government").

On a related note, it is critical that both the instructions and the enumerators be concise, clear, and uniform in their explanation of what information is being requested of each Native person being surveyed. Variations in local customs, practices, and cultural differences must be part of any federal survey being conducted, to ensure it is effective. That is precisely why supplemental studies, such as the planned Census Test on Tribal Lands, must be completed by federal agencies that will be conducting surveys of the AIAN population. It would be a travesty to have the 2020 Census Questionnaire tested in Indian County for the first time on Census Day in 2020.

Additional resources must be allocated for outreach to Indian Country:

It is a tremendous credit to the professionalism of Census staff that they have been actively engaged with tribal leaders and members to address issues impacting the enumeration in Indian Country through a series of tribal consultations in the ramp-up to the 2020 Census. Beginning in October 2015, the Census Bureau held tribal consultations at locations around the country.[90] One of the important results from those consultations was the Bureau's decision not to ask about tribal enrollment on the 2020 Census questionnaire.[91] The tribal consultations have helped bridge some of the gulf that separates the Tribes and Native peoples from the federal government. But those efforts must be ongoing to build on the nascent relationships that have developed. And equally important, those efforts must be funded by Congress.

In addition, more resources must be committed to outreach and partnership programs in Indian Country. Many of the elements proposed in the Census Bureau's Integrated Communications Plan to target the AIAN population will be ineffective in the most isolated parts of Indian Country. For example, the proposal identifies traditional modes of communication that are either completely unavailable in Indian Country or are inaccessible to large numbers of people.[92] Television and radio are not available to many Alaska Native communities and Indian reservations. For example, many of NARF's client villages in the Bethel, Dillingham, Kuslivak, and Yukon-Koyukak Census Areas reported that they receive no radio signals and instead have to rely on announcements being made over the village Citizens Band (CB) radio. Billboards, newspapers, and magazines likewise are not available or used in many places. Broadband access is non-existent on a majority of the tribal lands in rural areas. A "one-size-fits-all" approach, such as what is suggested in the Bureau's outreach planning, simply will not work in Indian Country.

The Census Bureau also does not have program funding in place to communicate in Native languages, despite the fact that English is not widely spoken or used in many parts of Indian Country. *The Bureau's services in non-English languages for past Census – as well as for the planned 2020 Census – do not include a single American Indian or Alaska native language.* All of the language services offered have been for Asian and European languages.[93] The Census Bureau intends to rely exclusively on "Partnership Efforts" to reach even widely used American Indian and Alaska Native languages, such as Navajo and Yup'ik.[94]

---

[90] *See* Tribal Consultations, *supra* note 67, at 2, 5.

[91] *See id.* at 11.

[92] *See* U.S. Census Bureau, Integrated Communications Plan (version 1.0) (June 2, 2017) ("Communications Plan"), *available at https://www2.census.gov/programs-surveys/decennial/2020/program-management/planning-docs/2020_integrated_COM_plan.pdf.*

[93] *See id.* at 74-77.

[94] *See id.* at 76-77.

Effective outreach and publicity in Indian Country requires a personal approach that will be tailored to the distinct cultural and linguistic needs of each Alaska Native village or reservation. Census publicity should be translated into Native languages and account for distinct dialectical differences through the use of the same methods that prove effective for language assistance in voting: translations by panels of qualified bilingual translators and confirmation of the quality of translations through testing among community members.

Outreach coordinators will need to be hired from village and tribal communities to identify, plan, and execute the most effective methods of communicating about the importance of the Census and how to ensure an accurate count is obtained. In some places, that may require making announcements over a CB radio. In other places, it might be to discuss the Census during tribal council meetings or other community gatherings. Tribal social service organizations can be engaged to disseminate information and answer questions.

These suggestions all require funding to tailor outreach and publicity campaigns to Native communities. It is understandable that there are efforts being undertaken to minimize costs associated with conducting federal surveys using race and ethnicity data. However, those efforts cannot come at the expense of accurate and complete measurements of the AIAN population. They also cannot require socio-economically disadvantaged Native villages and Tribes to bear the brunt of the burden and be compelled to engage in self-help to ensure they are counted. As one of the Hardest-to-Count populations, additional resources beyond those already allocated for the 2020 Census must be directed towards Indian Country.

Trusted American Indians and Alaska Natives should be enumerators:

The most frequent input on the Census that we have received during NAVRC's field hearings is that the enumeration on tribal lands should be conducted by Natives, not non-Natives. This issue came up in response to a proposal by the Census Bureau to use postal workers as enumerators. Postal workers in Indian Country often are non-Natives. The Bureau has considered employing postal workers to conduct the Census because, it was reasoned, they would most likely know where people live and could minimize some of the undercount for those with non-traditional mailing address.

American Indians and Alaska Natives have significant concerns about the postal worker proposal for a variety of reasons. They expressed extreme discomfort with the prospect of having to share some of their most personal and sensitive information (e.g., their ages, education and literacy levels, household income) with someone who they may see every day delivering mail. The consensus was that such an approach would likely discourage participation or accurate disclosure of information to Census enumerators. Moreover, because so many of AIAN people use non-traditional mailing methods such as post office or general delivery boxes shared by multiple families or generations of a single family, postal workers frequently will have no idea of how many people live in a particular household, or possibly even where the household is located. If the postal worker happens to be a non-Native, which many (and perhaps even most) would be, these concerns would be even greater.

The most accepted suggestion is that enumerators for each tribe or Native village should be hired from that tribe or village and not from the outside (including from other tribes or villages). Tribal leaders should be consulted to identify the people most trusted in their community to conduct an in-person enumeration. This approach would have the added benefits of using someone who already knows where people live and whose trusted reputation is more likely to lead to participation in the Census and elicit accurate responses.

Americans Indians and Alaska Natives should train enumerators in Indian Country:

Related feedback from tribal communities is that American Indians and Alaska Natives should be hired to prepare and provide all training for Census enumeration in Indian Country. As the earlier example highlights,[95] non-Native trainers who are training Native enumerators on how to be culturally sensitive in Indian Country are not well received. Nor are Census workers who wear suits when they conduct in-person training or door-to-door enumeration. Some of the best trainers to help prepare for Census 2020 can be readily drawn from Native professionals who work in tribal or community offices, or from among the local Native educators.

Census 2020 and the Bureau's leadership must be free of the taint of partisanship:

The Census Bureau and its leadership have, of necessity, been free of partisan taint in the Bureau's operations. The Bureau's mandate under Article I, Section 2 of the Constitution is to provide an accurate enumeration of all people in the United States, to ensure the proper apportionment among the several states. It has other surveying and data-gathering responsibilities under many federal statutes. To promote mandated compliance with its data-gathering efforts, it is essential that the American public have faith that Census Bureau leadership and professionals will perform their duties free of any partisanship or partisan influence.

Although the Deputy Director position does not require Senate confirmation, it nevertheless is critical to the fair and accurate functioning of the Census Bureau. The Deputy Director will oversee operational control over the 2020 Census. Historically, candidates to fill that position have been career statisticians who have many years of experience as Census Bureau employees. That approach has served the Bureau and the country well. The Census has been managed by neutral, impartial, non-partisan professionals who are intimately familiar with the Bureau's operations and are well-respected by Bureau staff. Through such exacting leadership, Census products are accepted and form the very cornerstone of the quality data that contributes to ensuring we have government representative of all the people. That tradition of non-partisanship and professionalism must continue, free from the political viewpoints of the person appointed to fill the Deputy Director position.

The same concerns hold true when the Administration selects its nominee for the Bureau's Director. It has now been over seven months since Director John Thompson resigned. Director Thompson, like his predecessors at the Bureau, performed his duties admirably and free of influence by any political party. Like the Deputy Director, any nominee who is named to fill

---

[95] *See supra* note 17 and accompanying text.

the Director vacancy must be a competent and experienced manager who has effectively overseen a statistical operation and who has the confidence of career Bureau staff and the American public to do so free of partisanship and political viewpoint.

Conclusion

Members of Congress and the leadership and professionals at the Census Bureau face many challenges in preparing for Census 2020. Those challenges are even greater in their collective efforts to ensure that all of the First Americans – American Indians and Alaska Natives – are fully and accurately counted. But they are not insurmountable.

NARF and its partners in the NAVRC look forward to working with this Committee to overcome the barriers to making Indian Country count in the 2020 Census. The data derived from the Census is too critical to all Americans – and Native Americans in particular – to undercount any population. It serves as the bedrock of our government, providing the population count used to determine the number of representatives each state will have, as well as the equal representation of voters in each community. It provides data that is critical to efforts to secure compliance with our civil rights laws. It is vital to offering tribal governments and Native peoples equal access to federal, state, and local funding that is essential to helping them to secure the American dream. In summary, we all need to work together to get the count right.

Thank you very much for your attention. I will welcome the opportunity to answer any questions you may have.

The CHAIRMAN. Thank you, Mr. Tucker.

We will now have five-minute rounds of questioning, which I will start.

I would like to start with you, Director Jarmin. How does the Census Bureau reconcile with BIA location, boundaries, and so forth on tribal lands, and, of course, that is necessary in terms of identifying your population counts? So how do you go through that process?

Mr. JARMIN. So, as I mentioned in my testimony, Senator, so what we do is we work with BIA, we work with the Tribes, we do the Annual Boundary Annexation Survey, where we send maps out to not just to tribal organizations, but to local governments across the Country to make sure that we get any changes in boundaries incorporated into our geographic systems as quickly as we can.

The CHAIRMAN. And is that a smooth process where you, by and large, have agreement, or is it contested?

Mr. JARMIN. Yes, it is, by and large, a smooth process.

The CHAIRMAN. Address, if you would for me, in some cases in tribal communities you have overcrowding and you may have multiple families living in one residence, and you may have movement, you know, in terms of where they live and so forth, temporary addresses and all those kinds of things. So, how do you get an accurate count in those situations?

Mr. JARMIN. That is a really good question, Senator. So, I think one of the things that we need to do better to strive to communicate to tribal communities is that there is sometimes a hesitancy to provide information about more than one family living in a particular house. The data that we collect are confidential and used for statistical purposes only, and perhaps could be used to make the case for more housing assistance if we could get a complete count.

So we need to make sure that our enumerators are trained to identify when it looks like there may be additional people in the house, to ask the right questions, to sort of suss out what the right count is. We just want to get the count; we don't provide that information to anybody other than ourselves, and it will be kept confidential.

The CHAIRMAN. Do you feel that you are getting through with that message and that you are getting people to come forward and be counted, versus, you know, what has been a reticence in some cases to provide information?

Mr. JARMIN. I do think there is some improvement that could be made, but we are successful some of the times; some of the times we are not successful. So I think more training, more focus on that particular issue will be helpful in 2020.

The CHAIRMAN. Ms. Gore, would you talk about how do we reach geographically isolated communities and what are some of the things that you think are successful and can be successful?

Ms. GORE. I would say there are a number of things. I would say, first of all, having a partnership specialist contacting them, they work within a region and can help with messaging and outreach, help the Tribes develop that. I think that is critically important. And in 2019 Census will begin developing complete count committees. Those also work on a regional basis, and it helps to educate those at the local level, number one, the importance, how to develop that cultural sensitivity in the messaging, how to conduct the outreach, who should be engaged, and really get the message out early, before census begins in 2020. That is what I would suggest.

Our State has already begun with an Alaska stakeholders meeting. We have begun our conversation by looking at 2010 and where our challenges were and informing Census, working with them to inform them where our challenges were as a State in those remote communities so that they could be prepared and we could work with them to get some of those challenges or barriers taken down before 2020.

I hope that answers your question, Chairman.

The CHAIRMAN. Yes. These partnership specialists, talk about them. How do you make sure you get good partnership specialists that can really get that job done?

Ms. GORE. Well, I can speak only for my State, and, in our region, we worked with Jamie Christy, who is the Regional Director out of Los Angeles, and he advertised for an Alaska Native to be that partnership specialist. He recognized that that was an opportunity for the State; that our hardest to count communities needed that representation, and, indeed, we have a representative that is Alaska Native, and we are pleased to have her.

The CHAIRMAN. Yes. I mean, you need somebody that can kind of connect, right?

Ms. GORE. Absolutely.

The CHAIRMAN. And break through some of the reticence, and to come forward and also that understands your State and how to work with people.

Ms. GORE. Absolutely. I would just say that Census was great at reaching out to us and asking us to help identify people that could apply for that position. So, the Census Bureau didn't just simply put out an ad; they did some outreach with those of us that had boots on the ground, and I sincerely appreciate that effort. It did bring some new names forward, and I appreciate that they took our recommendations, and we have, I think, a very good representative today.

Thank you.

The CHAIRMAN. And then just one other question for President Keel. How about technology? Have you seen things in the technology world that can really help on the Reservation?

Mr. KEEL. Absolutely. The outreach from tribal governments can put the word out, can get the sample ballots and sample types of documents out to the citizens is very helpful, but there is a problem, as has been noted. Not all communities have broadband, not all of our communities have access to the Internet, so that sometimes could be a problem. But the electronic and technology today does allow us to interact with our citizens a great deal more effectively.

The CHAIRMAN. Vice Chairman Udall.

Senator UDALL. Thank you.

Before I begin here, let me just thank President Keel on his inaugural address. I was there to hear it and it was excellent, and I think he really laid out a good agenda for Indian Country.

Mr. KEEL. And we thank you, too, Senator, for your response.

Senator UDALL. Well, thank you. Thank you very much.

Mr. KEEL. Thank you.

Senator UDALL. And we also have in the audience the Governor of the Laguna Pueblo, Virgil Siow. He is back there.

Virgil, good to see you. Welcome. Good to have you here on this issue.

One important area where the Administration's fiscal year 2019 budget falls short yet again is funding for the Census Bureau's partnership program, which entrusts local groups with promoting participation in Indian Country.

Mr. Jarmin, according to written testimony for this hearing, the Bureau lags far behind in hiring partnership staff. By some estimates, the Bureau has only hired about 40 partnership specialists. In 2010, the Bureau hired 3,800. And now we are hearing the Bureau only plans to hire 1,000.

Can you provide us an update on the Bureau's progress? And why would you hire less than a third from what you used in the last census, and you still, with all of those partnership people, had a 5 percent undercount?

Mr. JARMIN. Thank you, Vice Chairman, for the question. So, in our lifecycle cost estimate, which we worked very carefully with the secretary and department staff last year to sort of remap what the resources needs were going to be to get done to keep us on the critical path to completing a fair and accurate census, one of the things we looked at was the communication and partnership programs. We have $500 billion for the advertising program and about $248 billion for the partnership program. Those are both substantial increases over what we did in 2010.

For the partnership specialists, in particular, we had 800 of those in 2010, and the balance were what we call partnership assistants; and many of those were hired with money that came from the Recovery Act. So, this time we will be putting more partnership specialists on the ground. This is an area where you all can help us. I mean, we really need to have our fiscal year 2019 budget on time so that we can start that process in October. We will be probably starting, you know, posting some of those jobs over the summer so that we can kind of get people in the door and up and running as soon as we can. But, again, it is going to be, if we are on a CR again, that is going to put us off our timing a little bit.

Senator UDALL. Are you intending, with the assistants, to come up to about the same number as in 2010?

Mr. JARMIN. So, right now we do not have a plan to hire that many of the assistants, no.

Senator UDALL. Of the assistants.

Mr. JARMIN. Yes.

Senator UDALL. And didn't they help a lot in bringing the undercount down? I mean, if you go back to 1990, with a 12 percent undercount, so it seems to me we really need to focus on that.

But let me shift over here to President Keel. NCAI played a vital role during the last census with Indian Country counts. Can you discuss NCAI's plans for partnerships this next census?

Mr. KEEL. Thank you, Senator, for that question. Outreach to Indian Country is critical. In fact, NCAI did conduct a lot of outreach in 2010, and it is important that we do that again. We do as much as we can outreach to all of Indian Country to get the word out, but it is also critical and we want to add that census funding and policy issues, they cause us to shoulder a lot of the burden that at times puts a strain on our resources as well.

We do as much as we can to partner with them, and we will do our very best to get the word out to all of our communities, even those that are most remote, to make sure that they understand how important this is. But it does cause an inordinate amount of work on a limited number of staff.

Senator UDALL. Thank you.

The census can have a profound influence on the issue of voting accessibility, everything from a constituent's voting district to the availability of language assistance at the polls.

Mr. Tucker, can you please explain the importance of fully funding the data collection efforts as it relates to voting language assistance? And then I know you probably also have an opinion on this partnership specialists and whether they are sufficient in numbers, and you have heard Mr. Jarmin's testimony. Please go ahead.

Mr. TUCKER. Thank you, Senator. I will start off with the partnership program. Just by way of example, taking what Ms. Gore said about having one program specialist currently with five States, in your own home State currently, the Native language program that is in place, and Secretary Oliver's office has eight full-time employees, four of them who are bilingual—I am sorry, eight of whom are bilingual in four different Native languages. That is just for four counties that are largely in the northern part of the State.

So, the point to emphasize here is that the Census Bureau really does need more to be effective because it is a very big ask.

In terms of language assistance, turning to the American Community Survey briefly, the issue is that if you underfund it for even a single year, it can jeopardize the ability of the Census Bureau to make accurate language determinations, which are done on a rolling five-year basis.

And then, of course, the other part of voting and census is that the Public Law 97–141 data is the building block for everything that we do, whether it is apportionment, redistricting, or in instances in which organizations like NARF have to bring voting rights litigation, we need the data for both the voting blocks, as well as the socioeconomic data to demonstrate the violations.

Senator UDALL. Thank you, Mr. Tucker.

And I know, Ms. Gore, you made it really clear that you didn't think they were hiring enough partnership specialists at this particular point, and you pointed out what the Alaska situation was, so thank you.

Thank you, Mr. Chairman.

The CHAIRMAN. Senator Murkowski?

Senator MURKOWSKI. Thank you, Mr. Chairman. And I thank you for the focus on the partnership specialists, and, Carol, your testimony again given by way of example.

We all know that folks are prepared to work hard as we move towards the actual count, but you can only do as much as you can possibly do; and recognizing not only the human resource, but the resource behind the count is very important going forward.

I wanted to ask you, and, again, this is to you, Ms. Gore, when you responded to the Chairman when he asked about how you reach out to these very rural areas, you said that you looked to the 2010 Census and the count, and the lessons learned there.

From just that, your lessons learned, and let's use Alaska as a specific example, what are we doing with, again, some of these more remote communities that we didn't do in 2010? I want to hear a couple of the best practices that you are anticipating.

Ms. GORE. Sure. Thank you for the good question, Senator Murkowski. It is good to see you. I would say, first of all, lessons learned in 2010, we learned that boots on the ground really mattered; that the absence of boots on the ground in remote Alaska, I would say, and not just rural Alaska, where there is no infrastructure to get anyone in to some of our smaller communities except by plane or boat or a snow machine if you are there in January, was really, really critical.

Also, I would say engaging those communities in advance so that they were educated about the importance of census. There is almost nothing more important to our small communities than Federal funding, and when we are working with communities that have maybe less than 25 individuals living in a community, they need to be engaged, and they need to be engaged by tribal leaders who understand the importance of that. So having an earlier education has also mattered in remote and rural Alaska.

I would say, also engaging our Alaska Native regional corporations who can help to communicate. Using those partnerships has helped to save the Federal Government money because we have that early engagement. It is not just boots on the ground, but it is also communicating to Census that telecommunications is not going to work; we have to have paper methods to communicate with people that live in remote and rural Alaska.

We know that broadband is not there yet; we know they don't have accessibility. Sometimes we can't even apply for a grant on a timely basis because there is no place through which to work on an online system.

So those are some of the examples I would use, and I am sure they are shared by other remote and rural communities in the lower 48 States, we call them.

Thank you for that question.

Senator MURKOWSKI. I appreciate that and I appreciate your last point about having a hard copy.

It is actually pretty fortuitous, Mr. Chairman, because just last week I was the designated resident of this particular address here in Washington, D.C. I received the American Community Survey. I was randomly chosen. I was told that my response is required by law. And I looked at it and it says I am supposed to complete this survey online as soon as possible at respond.census.gov/acs. I am sorry, I wasn't going to fill this out online; I wasn't going to do it. And then I get to the next line, the next paragraph that says, "If you are unable to complete the survey online, there is no need to contact us; we will send you a paper questionnaire in a few weeks." So, being the good taxpayer that I am, I am waiting for my paper questionnaire.

I did get a follow-up just yesterday. This is very fortuitous, Mr. Chairman. Just yesterday I got a message from the Director of the U.S. Census Bureau, who reminded me that I should have received my instructions once again to go online, and I am required by law to do it.

Now, I am not too worried, but I do worry about some of our seniors in our very remote areas who look at this and say, my gosh, my response to this is required by law, and I have to do it by going online. I don't have to do it by going online; I can wait.

But I do think that this is, again, one of these examples where we need to make sure that we are reaching people the way that they can be reached; and many people cannot be reached, or don't want to communicate, by the Internet, so making sure that we have this hard copy. So I am awaiting that, and then at that point in time I will be that resident at this household who will comply, but until then, don't expect me to do it online.

I do want to ask, and I know that my time has expired here, but as we are collecting these, these are randomly assigned to households. Do we, in these random assignments, is there equal emphasis on rural and outlying areas as there is in urban centers? Do you know, Mr. Jarmin?

Mr. JARMIN. Well, thanks for the question, Senator Murkowski, and we really appreciate you filling out your ACS. As you heard, the data are critical.

Senator MURKOWSKI. Yes. I will get to it.

Mr. JARMIN. And we do do it electronically and we try to encourage people to do it electronically because we get better data. It is easier for us to process and it provides the extra resources that we might need to really reach out to the folks who can't do it online, so it is important that the people who can fill it out in the most efficient and high quality manner.

Senator MURKOWSKI. You might convince me to do it online to save you money.

[Laughter.]

Mr. JARMIN. So the ACS is a stratified survey where we try to make sure that we can publish statistics for certain areas, so some rural areas may be oversampled for us to be able to publish data for a rural area. So you might get a higher sampling rate amongst a community where there it is less dense. So it does impose a slightly higher burden, but we can't publish data if we don't do that; we just wouldn't be able to publish data for many communities in Alaska or the American West if we didn't do that.

Senator MURKOWSKI. I understand.

Thank you, Mr. Chairman. Thank you all.

The CHAIRMAN. Senator Murkowski, that was excellent. Nothing like a concrete example to know what we are dealing with. And I agree with you 100 percent. I mean, obviously, most people do it online, but I think having that backup and saying, hey, if you don't want to do it online, you know, a paper copy is coming. Very important and point really well made.

Senator Smith.

STATEMENT OF HON. TINA SMITH,
U.S. SENATOR FROM MINNESOTA

Senator SMITH. Thank you, Chair Hoeven and Vice Chair Udall, and thank you all very much for being here today. I have a couple of questions for Mr. Jarmin.

As Senator Heitkamp observed, and I think also President Keel, these field tests for the new procedures for administrating the census in Indian territories and Indian communities were cancelled due to lack of funding, so I am wondering if you can just tell us a little bit about the consequences of this. Was the Bureau able to salvage anything from that process that might be incorporated into kind of where we go from here?

Mr. JARMIN. Well, thank you, Senator Smith. So, we did not take that decision lightly. We designed those tests; we intended to carry them out. There was some budget uncertainty, as my fellow witnesses attested to, so we needed to make a decision that we thought could best keep us on the critical path to the census.

We weren't testing any procedures that were particularly new in Indian Country. Obviously, for all the reasons that have been stated, we do plan to have lots of boots on the ground; we do plan to use a lot of the traditional methods and to rely really heavily on partnership and outreach to sort of get the word out and drive response.

But one thing that we were disappointed that we were not able to test was our systems in areas of low connectivity, so our field staff will be using an iPhone when they go out. That needs to work both in the connected and a disconnected state. So we were able to, in the 18 end-to-end test, which is ongoing right now, the address canvassing part of that that occurred last fall, we were able to test a lot of that in West Virginia, which had a large area that had limited connectivity as well, and partly in Pierce County,

Washington. So we were able to test those systems, so we were able to salvage a good part of what we really wanted to learn, but, again, it was a decision that we made that we thought gave us the best opportunity to be successful.

Senator SMITH. Well, thank you. And I want to be clear I have a lot of respect for the professionals at the Census Bureau; the question is whether you have the resources and what you need to be able to do your job.

So, this brings me to another thing I am kind of concerned about. We are expecting to have, I understand, three area offices in Minnesota for the 2020 Census; one in Duluth, one in Minneapolis, and one in the Rochester area. But we won't be able to have any offices in basically the western two-thirds of the State, where many of our largest Native communities are. These offices will be hundreds of miles away from places like White Earth and Red Lake, and other places.

So, can you help me, can you just talk a little bit about whether there is any chance, how are we going to best serve this vast area? It is a lot if you are in Minnesota, but I think about the challenges that Senator Murkowski will have in Alaska dwarf this in many ways. But could you just talk a little about what we can do about this, if anything?

Mr. JARMIN. So I do think that our plan for staffing the field offices and how that is going to manage down to the enumerator in this census is going to allow us to have a much less dense area office network, and a lot of that is because we are not going to have as many sort of face-to-face meetings. Work will be doled out on a daily basis to enumerators in an automated fashion, as opposed to getting paper lists and stuff like that from your field supervisor, so I think we are pretty confident we will be able to address that. Obviously, if more would be margin would be a little bit better, but I don't know if it would really justify the cost.

Senator SMITH. One of the things we are doing in Minnesota, and it sounds like it might be similar to what you are working on, Ms. Gore, in Alaska, is really developing a Minnesota-specific communications plan for the census, and we are specifically working to engage American Indian communities in that process early on. I think that was a best practice that you identified, Ms. Gore, as we were thinking about this, and I am really hopeful that this will help us.

In Minnesota, we had one of the higher report rates in the Country, at 81 percent, which is typical of my State; we like to do what we are supposed to do. But the rates dropped to the mid-50s in our Native American communities and surrounding counties. So I am glad that we kind of like think about what these best practices are and maybe also incorporate them at the Federal level also.

Thank you very much, Mr. Chair.

The CHAIRMAN. Senator Cortez Masto.

STATEMENT OF HON. CATHERINE CORTEZ MASTO, U.S. SENATOR FROM NEVADA

Senator CORTEZ MASTO. Thank you. Thank you, Mr. Chair and Ranking Member Udall.

Welcome to everyone. Thank you for being here.

Mr. Tucker, welcome, from Las Vegas, I understand. Welcome here. That is fantastic.

Mr. TUCKER. Thank you.

Senator CORTEZ MASTO. President Keel, I would like to ask you a question. It has been widely reported that the DOJ requested that the Census Bureau include a question on citizenship in its 2020 Census, and I joined a letter in January with Senator Feinstein and some of my other Senate colleagues to Secretary Wilbur Ross expressing serious concerns about the DOJ's request. I have expressed my deep concern about this at the Senate Commerce Committee hearings as well, and have been deeply troubled by reports of minority populations being significantly underenumerated. In fact, this is a problem that we know happens in the Latino communities, where 400,000 young Latino children ages 0 to 4 were uncounted in 2010, including 6,000 in Clark County, Nevada.

Under the current Administration, immigrants and minority groups are fearful for the security and safety of their families, and the inclusion of a question on citizenship could impact the accuracy of the census and its data. Given this Administration's rhetoric and actions relating to immigrants and minority groups, the DOJ request on a question on citizenship is alarming.

You note in your testimony, President Keel, that NCAI opposes the citizenship question in the census. Can you elaborate about NCAI's concerns that such a question would suppress participation in the census?

Mr. KEEL. Well, thank you, Senator, for that question. I think it goes back to what we spoke about earlier, and in our testimony we talk about the mistrust and the historic misrepresentation or how this data could be possibly used. So I think when we talk about the cynicism or the mistrust or distrust of the forms are those forms themselves, and I think you mentioned just a moment ago about the Latino and the other populations, the Native populations have those same fears and those same cynical responses, I believe.

Senator CORTEZ MASTO. Right.

Mr. Tucker, do you have anything to add to that?

Mr. TUCKER. I would agree with President Keel. In fact, it is very interesting, because just turning to the State of Nevada, for example, we conducted a study of four States, including Nevada, examining how did American Indians feel towards the Federal, State, and local governments.

Nevada actually had the highest level of trust in the Federal Government, but it was 28 percent. And what we see consistently across Indian Country, regardless of which part of Indian Country we are talking about, is Native Americans believe a lot more and have a lot more trust in their own tribal governments than they do in any non-tribal government. So, I would agree that any asking of a citizenship question just erects another barrier that in all likelihood is just going to make more people not want to participate and, frankly, not report accurately.

Senator CORTEZ MASTO. Right. Thank you.

Mr. Tucker, let me stay with you. In your testimony, you observe that a fair and accurate census and a comprehensive American Community Survey must be considered among the most significant civil rights issue facing the Country today. This is something I hear every day when I engage with my Tribes across the State; and, in fact, a constituent wrote to me about the hardship many Shoshone and Paiute people endure just to vote, and she just wrote "Many indigenous people live on the Duckwater Reservation and have to drive a long way to vote."

I want her to know that our Native American people count, that we see them, we are listening to them. My question to you is an accurate and accessible census is a constitutional responsibility, and I am proud to work on this Committee to ensure its accuracy. Can you, though, please discuss the importance of census data in light of the Supreme Court's Shelby County decision and the increased necessity of litigation to challenge unlawful Native vote suppression?

Mr. TUCKER. It is a great question and it is very timely, again, because we are coming up on, I believe it is, the fifth anniversary of Shelby County. So, in terms of what Native groups have to do through groups such as NARF, we are having to bring a lot more Section 2 cases, which are the general nondiscrimination provisions under the Voting Rights Act. To do that, it is heavily dependent on census data.

Two of the three Gingles preconditions to establishing vote dilution rely directly on census data, geographical compactness and racial bloc voting. And then, of course, the other piece of it is the Senate factors. Many of the Senate factors to establish a violation require socioeconomic data and data that basically shows that Native candidates who have to compete in a very, very large district may be economically disadvantaged and can't do that.

But the best example actually comes from Nevada, from just before the 2016 election. In the case of Sanchez v. Cegavske, it actually involved a situation where four Tribes in the northern part of Nevada sued the State of Nevada and some of the counties because of distance issues in order to get to voter registration and in-person voting; and there the critical component that we needed from Census was to show lack of access to reliable transportation in households and what the impact on socioeconomically disadvantaged groups was in trying to drive distances, such as, for example, when you talk about Duckwater in Nye County, they are very, very great distances and they do have a disenfranchising effect.

Senator CORTEZ MASTO. Thank you.

I notice my time is up. Thank you so much for being here today and the discussion.

The CHAIRMAN. Vice Chairman Udall?

Senator UDALL. Thank you, Mr. Chairman.

As we all know, the census is a critically important government function, and yet the current Administration has yet to nominate a qualified candidate to lead the Census Bureau in the critical years leading up to 2020. That is not to in any way disparage the career folks that are out there; they spend a lot of time working on this, I know. And I find this problematic for a number of reasons, including a lack of accountability.

I take my oversight duties very seriously and want to ensure we have a successful 2020 Census, one that is data-driven and free of politics.

President Keel, do you see this leadership vacuum as a problem leading up to the 2020 Census?

Mr. KEEL. Thank you, Senator Udall. Leadership at the Census Bureau is critical to the success of the census. When you say a leadership vacuum, we believe that it is important that we have strong leadership, and it is important for the whole direction. When you talk about how we conduct the census and how it is understood and received in Indian Country, as well as across the Country, I believe it is important that we get strong leadership in place now so that we can move forward.

Senator UDALL. President Keel, I share your concern over reports that the Department of Justice requested the Census Bureau include a question on citizenship, a proposal that the National Congress of American Indians oppose. I oppose injecting politics into the census with these types of questions, which will likely have a chilling effect on communities that are already at risk of being undercounted, and I share that concern.

Mr. Tucker, there have been additional reports of highly partisan candidates to senior roles at the Census Bureau and the Department of Commerce. Is this cause for concern for you with respect to ensuring that the census is done accurately and fairly?

Mr. TUCKER. It is, Senator, for two reasons. One, as many of you have already discussed, this is a constitutional mandate under Article I, Section 2 of the Constitution, and it has to be free of any sort of outlook that it could be tilting, you know, the count in favor of one party or another, or undercounting any particular group to favor one party or the other.

The other issue is partisanship undermines the public faith that folks have in the Bureau; and, in doing that, that leads to the very sort of chilling effect that President Keel talked about. We don't want to make hard-to-count populations even harder to count either through partisan leadership or through questions such as a citizenship question that may make people more reluctant to participate.

Senator UDALL. President Keel, did you have a comment on the citizenship question?

Mr. KEEL. I was going to add that the Census Bureau has already developed and sent out questionnaires that are designed to answer those questions, so putting another question there just seems duplicative and more costly.

Senator UDALL. As I understand it, the message to the Census Bureau from tribal delegates has been loud and clear: hire and train locally. That means hiring trusted individuals from within each community to do everything from outreach to actual enumeration.

Mr. Jarmin, what is the Bureau's plan for hiring American Indians and Alaska Natives from within each community? I think that one of the things that has come out here is are there going to be enough to reach these smaller areas, like others have talked about, where you have a community of 25 who may be very suspicious of strangers and outsiders, and somebody that knows them may be able to go in there and get a good count and encourage people to come forward with the information.

Mr. JARMIN. Well, thanks, Vice Chairman Udall. Our plan definitely not only in Indian Country, but across the Country, is to hire enumerators who are representative of the communities that we are going to have them enumerating in, for many reasons, for trust, for language proficiency. It is absolutely critical to have a successful census that the people who are knocking on doors are people that households will open the doors to and can communicate with efficiently, so that is our plan. We will be working with the Tribes to identify not just the people who are going to do the knocking, but the people who are going to do the hiring, the local management, all tiers of the field staff.

Senator UDALL. Thank you.

Senator Hoeven and I are both appropriators, and we take very seriously what you say in terms of when you get to 2019, have the budget in place. The positive thing for you is that we have a number now for 2019, and we should be able to work and get them a budget at the beginning of the fiscal year so that you can be prepared and get people out there.

Thank you.

Mr. JARMIN. We would be very appreciative of that, and anything that we can do to help you in that, just let us know.

Senator UDALL. Okay. Thank you.

The CHAIRMAN. Senator Cortez Masto, any other questions?

Senator CORTEZ MASTO. No.

The CHAIRMAN. Okay, if there are no more questions, members may also submit follow-up written questions for the record, and the hearing record will be open for two weeks.

Again, I want to thank the witnesses for your time and your testimony. We appreciate it very much.

This hearing is adjourned.

[Whereupon, at 4:08 p.m., the hearing was concluded.]

A P P E N D I X

PREPARED STATEMENT OF HON. BILL JOHN BAKER, PRINCIPAL CHIEF, CHEROKEE NATION

Dear Chairman Hoeven, Vice Chairman Udall and Committee Members:

On behalf of Cherokee Nation, please accept the following comments for the record to the United States Senate Committee on Indian Affairs oversight hearing on "Making Indian Country Count: Native Americans and the 2020 Census." Cherokee Nation is the largest federally recognized Indian tribe in the United States with almost 360,000 citizens worldwide and with approximately 275,000 of those citizens residing in Oklahoma. Our tribal headquarters is located in Tahlequah, Oklahoma, and the tribe's jurisdiction covers most or all of 14 counties in northeastern Oklahoma and equals about 7,000 square miles.

Accurate census data is crucial to ensure Cherokee Nation receives the appropriate funds for health, housing, infrastructure and other essential community programs. In the past, inaccurate and outdated census data has inhibited Cherokee Nation's ability to strategically plan for both short-term and long-term funding for key tribal programs. Additionally, Census geographies routinely fail to capture adequately data on Cherokee Nation citizens who reside within the territorial jurisdiction of the Nation.

Recognizing the shortcomings in the data previously collected, Cherokee Nation has taken many proactive steps to ensure the 2020 Census correctly reflects the Cherokee population residing within the tribal government's territorial jurisdiction. In addition to participating in the Census Bureau's 2020 Census Tribal Consultations with Oklahoma Tribes, Cherokee Nation also reached out to the U.S. Census Bureau to participate in the Local Update of Census Addresses (LUCA) program.

LUCA is the only opportunity offered to tribal, state, and local governments to review and comment on the U.S. Census Bureau's residential address list for their jurisdiction prior to the 2020 Census. Unfortunately, *only* those federally recognized tribes with a reservation and/or off-reservation trust lands are eligible to participate. This limitation impedes Cherokee Nation's ability to participate in the LUCA program. In Oklahoma, the U.S. Census Bureau created Oklahoma Tribal Statistical Areas (OTSA) to represent reservations, as they existed prior to statehood. Therefore, because the U.S. Census Bureau does not recognize Oklahoma tribal land bases as "reservations" it does not allow any of the Oklahoma tribes, including the Cherokee Nation, to participate in the LUCA program. Instead, Cherokee Nation must submit its comments regarding the U.S. Census Bureau's address list prior to the 2020 Census to the State of Oklahoma who then submits the Nation's comments to the U.S. Census Bureau.

The opportunity to review and comment on prior census data is particularly important to Cherokee Nation in light of the U.S. District Court for Washington D.C.'s recent ruling in *Cherokee Nation v. Nash, et. al.* In its August 30, 2017 Order, the Court issued a long awaited ruling determining the rights and interests of Cherokee Freedmen descendants. The Court ruled that Freedmen descendants have the right to citizenship within the Cherokee Nation. Cherokee Nation has been processing Freedmen citizenship applications and anticipate more than 6,000 Freedmen citizens by with be enrolled as Cherokees by 2020.

Requiring Cherokee Nation to submit its comments through the State is an affront to our inherent sovereign rights as a government. The Census Bureau does not dispute the legal status of Cherokee Nation's land base. Rather, the OTSA designation was given in an attempt to give tribes meaningful data about the people who live on their lands. If the U.S. Census Bureau were to map tribal trust lands in Oklahoma, then Cherokee Nation would be able to participate in the LUCA program. Moreover, if trust lands were mapped, tribes could also participate in the Boundary Annexation Survey (BAS), an annual geography program through which tribes can review and update legal geographies. In the alternative, a change in policy to allow any federally recognized tribes to directly apply to LUCA, despite the land base classification, would benefit those tribes by allowing them to directly ensure the accuracy of their funding, and thus help to ensure that federal trust responsibilities are better met.

Thank you for your time and consideration in this matter.